John Garmo

Lifestyle WORSHIP

John Garmo

THOMAS NELSON PUBLISHERS
Nashville

Published in Nashville, Tennessee, by Thomas Nelson, Inc., Publishers, and
distributed in Canada by Word Communications, Ltd., Richmond, British
Columbia, and in the United Kingdom by Word (UK), Ltd., Milton Keynes,
England.

Library of Congress Cataloging-in-publication Data
Garmo, John.
    Lifestyle worship / John Garmo.
       p. cm.
    Includes bibliographical references.
    ISBN 0-8407-4897-3
    1. Vocation. Worship. 3. Pastoral theology. 4. Spiritual life—Christianity.
5. Garmo, John. I. Title
BV4740.G37   1993
248.4—dc20   93-24723
                                  CIP

Printed in the United States of America
1 2 3 4 5 6 7 - 98 97 96 95 94 93

DEDICATION

To Jan, my precious, patient wife,
   whose faithful, gentle, loving life
   belauds the Master's touch;

And to Byron, Krista, and Kara, our three,
   who bring deep joy to Jan and me
   — we love you kids so much! —

Here's my dream, my goal, the beat of my heart,
   my prayer for our family, as His works of art:

May Jesus Christ be praised.

Contents

❦

PART 1:
GROWING DEEPER

He is like a tree
  planted by streams of water,
which yields its fruit in season
  and whose leaf does not wither.
Whatever he does prospers.
  (Psalm 1:3)

Chapter 1

Changing Seasons

❧

Winter is tough on trees. Sometimes—especially in deep winter—a tree can seem a barren and forsaken relic. That it will ever recover its earlier health, beauty, and fruitfulness appears hopeless.

Yet it survives, in defiance of its harsh and bleak surroundings. How? A slow-moving, energizing flow of nourishment, encased by its coarse, disreputable bark, enables that tree not only to endure but also to flourish again in its season.

Have you ever felt that bitter cold, penetrating chill? I remember when it was *my* turn to be one of those winter-ravaged trees.

Changing Plans

It began the day after Easter. As I drove to my office that morning, I welcomed the effect April was having on our homey Midwestern town. *It won't be long now,* I reflected, *until spring awakens the landscape and transforms this barren, cold, slushy mess into grassy, warm, dry ground.*

Hurray! I'll store the snow shovel! I'll get reprieve from the ten minutes I spend bundling up for that thirty-second walk from the building to the car. Having grown up on the balmy West Coast, I welcomed spring each Midwestern year almost as if it were the Second Coming.

It sobered me momentarily to realize that what I witnessed in nature resembled the seasons of my life. The past six years had been tough.

They began when I left a secure college faculty position to pursue a demanding doctorate in an innovative field of study. My decision required not only a change of focus, but also a change of location. Gamely, Jan and I sold our house and moved our two young ones up to the Pacific Northwest.

Since I still had my family to support, I was glad that God also opened the door to my first full-time music pastorate. Having served for about a decade as a part-time church music leader, I welcomed the opportunity for more attention to this ministry.

The prospect of this double challenge was stimulating. For those who enjoy Scrabble, being able to do both the Ph.D. and the music pastorate was like Scrabbling on a triple-word-score!

Over the next six years of study, my entrepreneurial spirit drove me to develop the first such ministry in three successive churches. Each of those stints required another round of energy and stress: sell our old house; buy a new one; move our family and belongings; and establish new relationships, new routines, and a new work culture.

God also blessed us with a growing family. Two years into the program, Kara added her smiling face to those of Byron and Krista, giving Jan three energetic lambs to shepherd. Early on in our marriage, Jan and I had agreed that we wanted her, rather than a day-care center, to mother our kids. With that decision, we commissioned her principally, though not exclusively, to home ministry and committed ourselves to one humble income.

Having thus planned the work, the next stage was to work the plan.

Changing Pressures

Academically, the pressure increased as the program progressed. It was like climbing a mountain that got steeper as I got weaker. Each ridge I conquered brought a moment of celebration coupled with a tired-but-determined look at the next challenge on the horizon.

Days off from work were often spent in research-related activity. Evenings, after romping with the kids, were spent likewise.

I continually struggled to compress the generous study time that most of my doctoral program colleagues enjoyed into the comparatively meager study time I had available. The difficulty of grasping new concepts—and the possibility of failure—was much more acute. Perhaps you've been there and know what I mean.

Meanwhile, our church ministry was both exhilarating and exhausting. Leading and managing were constant, though enjoyable, challenges: evaluating potential; budgeting for growth; bringing people together; keeping people committed; sharing vision ownership; planning, executing, and evaluating programs; and pastoring individuals as well as groups.

Other pressures surfaced as well. Though we lived thriftily, every thirty days we faced the threat of more month than money. Furthermore, our concern deepened as we watched my parents, far away in Southern California, progressively lose their hold on health. Our inability to be of any help to them was an increasing frustration as well.

A minister with these responsibilities counts heavily on his church board for personal and professional support. My belated discovery that their backing was not wholehearted, therefore, was deeply troubling.

Inner tension cranked up notch after notch as I shouldered these burdens and still tried to maintain some sense of balance in my life. I was close to personal limits I had never thought existed.

Yet, a profound rightness about what we did was there even amid the overwhelming schedule. Jan and I had not expected it to be easy, but we knew this situation was temporary. We figured we could outlast it.

In fact, we were not only surviving but we were accomplishing what we set out to do. Our sustaining hope was the expectation that God would use us—and what we learned or developed from our experience—for His glory.

It's winter now, but spring is comin', I told myself doggedly. My doctorate now verged on completion, and my new church ministry in the Midwest again developed ahead of schedule. Things were going well, and it wouldn't be long until I could relax my intense pace.

Or so I thought.

Chapter 2
Turning Points

❧

On that April day after Easter, I parked our station wagon and playfully jumped mud puddles on my path to the office building I shared with several others of our pastors. Inside, I chatted briefly with secretaries and colleagues as I soaked in the room's welcome warmth.

I was on an emotional high, fueled partially by the incoming change of weather and partially by the outgoing Easter season. Our Easter musical, performed in a nearby college auditorium, had been tiring but delightful, complete with choir, orchestra, drama, and multimedia.

The sight and sound of all those talented people working together so diligently was stimulating. The resulting sense of worship expressed by so many made me almost forget the tremendous effort invested to make it look so easy!

Settled into my office, I sorted out priorities for the week. I needn't have bothered; my priorities were soon dramatically arranged for me.

Mid-morning, my intercom buzzed. The senior pastor was on the other end of the line, asking if he could come in to see me. Certainly. In itself, that was not earth-shaking, but I somehow sensed that this would not be a casual fireside chat. Ever had *that* feeling?

Sure enough, after pleasantries were exchanged, he got to the point. In moments I found my inward self pulling back in shock, recoiling emotionally from nicely phrased words carrying a searing message.

They blurred, at times not even registering in my stunned brain. Some phrases floated up to the surface. "We think your gifts can be better used elsewhere. . . . Look for another place to work. . . . Nothing personal, of course. . . . You just don't fit here. . . ."

The pit of my stomach felt as if I had swallowed a chunk of ice the size of a hand grenade—whole. Then it exploded, giving my entire midsection a deep chill.

After he left my office, I called Jan and numbly relayed the tidings. She responded as the precious partner she is: no hysteria, no tantrums; just support, quietness, and love. It was just what I needed most.

When the Going Gets Tough...

I took some time to mentally retrace my ministry path. What had I done to deserve this?

Life up to then had basically been a steady string of successes. Not that I was born with a silver spoon in my mouth; rather, I grew up with the understanding that the person who worked hard and did well would be rewarded.

The blow of being asked to resign was therefore compounded—it seemed the reverse of what was deserved. Being asked to leave my work was a new experience; I had left positions in the past, but always at my initiative, always to take on a new challenge. This did not make sense, and, of course, it did not change the fact that I was suddenly "out."

And that's the way it was. Instead of a return to blessed normalcy after six years of steep mountain-climbing, year seven became our toughest test yet.

Within a few weeks, I was awarded my hard-earned Ph.D.—a major success—and was dismissed from a much-enjoyed ministry—a major failure. Whiplashed by emotions, the latter overwhelmed the former.

After the initial shock, I became optimistic. Many friends on the West Coast would know what openings might suit my background, right? This could be my chance to return and help my parents in Southern California!

Challenged and confident, I first contacted colleagues who were "in the know." Weeks and a barrage of calls and letters went by.

I was no closer to a new position anywhere along the West Coast. One lead after another evaporated like a desert mirage.

Puzzled and poor, I numbly and humbly began searching for work of *any* kind in our local area. No success: I was either over- or under-qualified for every reasonable and unreasonable job I explored. More weeks passed. Winter was ravaging my tree.

Dejected and destitute, I finally stood in line at the unemployment office. Even there I was rejected: Because our church was not a contributor to the system, no financial assistance was available for me.

In deepening despondency, and with no other alternative, I took my wagon directly to the welfare office.

Again I stood awkwardly in a barely moving line of people, afraid of being recognized and certain they were all staring at me behind my back. I felt like a hunk of beef hooked to a conveyor belt.

When I finally got to the counter, rejection mocked me once more. We had no money, yet our old station wagon had just enough resale value to prevent our receiving financial help.

I laughed at the irony of it, asking the clerk if I sold my only means of transportation to any possible job and wasted the proceeds on booze, would I then qualify for welfare assistance? "Yes," she replied.

I couldn't trust myself to say a word. I left, shaking my head in disbelief and carrying my self-esteem in a sling. "Lord?" I asked in confusion. "Is this what I get for doing what I thought You wanted me to do?"

Driven to Deeper Living

In defiance of this harsh, bleak winter, God was not asleep and I knew it. Throughout this experience, His nurture continued its quiet flow. Slowly, surely, steadily, and in a thousand ways He gave grace.

Not the least of these was to and through Jan. On the morning I got the word from my boss, she "got the Word" from God. Unaware of my impending news on that April morning, she read during her morning devotional: "He will have no fear of bad news; his heart is steadfast, trusting in the LORD" (Psalm 112:7).

Later in the morning when I conveyed our problem, Jan conveyed His promise. Her steadfast heart and trust in the Lord soothed and encouraged me. Isn't God's Spirit timely? Isn't His Word amazing? And what a treasure it is to have a godly wife!

Another evidence of His grace in Jan was her ingenuity. While I scoured the area for work, she scoured the area for food. She discovered a place that distributed surplus bread and dairy goods to needy people. Modern manna! We gratefully participated in that program.

Yet, as I pictured her standing in a parking lot line, waiting for handouts, I cannot express the failure and uselessness I felt as a husband, father, and ex-breadwinner. As trees go, I was bare-leaved, gnarled, fruitless, ugly—and the stream beside me was frozen solid.

I had several response options available: Fight the dismissal, stir up personal support, discredit my discreditors, etc.

Some of that might have been perversely enjoyable to do. Clearly, though, nothing would be gained and much could be lost in terms of ministry and organizational intangibles. I filtered those choices out.

Another option was bitterness. Bitterness, though, is an emotional cancer that can kill the carrier. That was and is too big a risk to take.

There was also the anger option. Frankly, I didn't have enough energy left over from job hunting for that.

I could have become sick. God was gracious.

I could have run away in despair. That, of course, would have added to the problem.

I might have run away spiritually, turning my back on faith in God. Thanks to His Spirit in my heart, I knew that I couldn't do that. In fact, the essence of faith is *holding on* when the situation is shaky.

Short of that was the possibility of becoming profoundly depressed. In truth, I was depressed. Not to the point of inactivity, but I was deeply sobered and slowly sinking into the quicksand of perceived worthlessness.

Yet, by the grace of God, what could have happened to us didn't.

Why not? As I look back on that winter wilderness experience, I see God driving us to deeper living. In His compassion, God sustained us through that time.

His Word

First, God took us to His Word. Long before this crisis, we knew that His love letter to us was "a lamp to [our] feet and a light for [our] path" (Ps. 119:105).

As I moved forward into my winter, God led me to look at two lifelong Bible heroes. I empathized with Joseph when, after depending on his brothers, they dumped him and sold him to an unknown future.

I pondered his dogged godliness while far away from supportive family and friends. He habitually demonstrated integrity of character and excellence in work—even though rewarded time after time with indifference or disgrace.

His reaction trumpeted his conviction: *With God in control, our response is more important than our situation.* I wanted to reflect that same sense of devotion and worship.

I identified with David when, as a fugitive, he sought food for himself and his family of followers. I understood more fully what he must have experienced as he willingly passed up opportunities to discredit King Saul. Using David's positive example, God helped me recognize my natural, retaliatory impulses as they were: self-gratifying and counter-productive.

Can you imagine what Joseph and David must have thought during their dark days? Discovered in the wide open spaces of obscurity, amid flocks of dull-witted sheep, God gives them each a dramatic and life-changing revelation of their bright and prominent futures. Horizons expand, expectancies ascend, and rekindled imaginations run wild.

Suddenly—bam!—they are jolted rudely from reverie to reality. Their brothers turn on them. They become outcasts. Instead of being lifted up in exaltation, they both come crashing down, Humpty Dumpty style.

"Lord?" they each must have asked in confusion. "Is this what I get for doing what I thought You wanted me to do?" Their determination to honor God in spite of discouraging circumstances became a standard against which I would gauge myself.

His People

Second, God sustained us through special people. Jan and I determined not to cause dissension within the church by talking to people about our predicament. Certain friends, however, sensed the situation and helped us in creative, simple, significant, wonderful ways.

Jan kept a journal of these blessings so we would not later forget God's nourishment during our winter wilderness experience. Some excerpts, eliminating names to preserve the anonymity of these encouraging human angels, will help explain God's care. They may give you some ideas of ways you can help any friends of yours who go through similar difficulties:

On Friday, Oct. 5th, Skip went down to apply for welfare . . . . It really hit me when he was gone how near we were to the bottom financially and I cried out to God in desperation. That morning's mail brought a check for $100 from _____. The next morning, the _____ called to ask if they could unload a few of their "surplus" groceries on us. I said, "Sure!"

_____ brought over three bags of groceries plus $50 and two new shirts for Skip.

On Monday, Oct. 8th, _____ brought over an anonymous gift for $250. While they were here, _____ brought over another check . . . . Together they were enough to pay our taxes . . . . The same day, _____ gave us a bag of groceries. She was cleaning out her refrigerator for their five-week trip. She also gave us a bag of apples.

_____ took us to the missions banquet and loaded our freezer with meat: five packages of hamburger, two roasts and one round steak package!!

_____babysat for us with no charge, and so did _____.

_____ put $50 in our mailbox the day we had to get glasses for Byron .... God was taking care of every need. The glasses cost $59 ...._____ gave Byron a free eye exam for his prescription.

Sat. eve. _____ [a widow with two children of her own] brought over a bag of apples, crackers and milk; also ingredients for meat loaf. And coffee.

Another cherished, unedited, heart-revealing entry recalls an envelope slipped to us by Krista, who was seven years old at the time. In it was this note: "This is money for you! You can use it intill dad gets his job. I love you. From Krista." With the note was $1.76 in cash: the little one's mite; her entire life savings.

The journal goes on for pages. Some friends from our college days, living far off in another state, heard we were in need and sent us several hundred dollars with no questions asked, and just when we needed it. Family and friends alike showed their love and support.

These kindnesses broke through the gloomy overcast like scattered rays of brilliant sunshine. They brought a profound assurance of God's personal love for us.

With that assurance of His personal love came a confidence in His personal care—even though, unquestionably, I was bewildered about the details. I had no idea how things would work out, but I had no question that they would work out.

As I ponder that period again, my heart erupts in the praise of Lamentations 3:22-23, "Because of the LORD's great love we are not consumed, for his compassions never fail. They are new every morning; great is your faithfulness."

PART 2: STRETCHING HIGHER

Therefore, I urge you, brothers,
in view of God's mercy,
to offer your bodies as living sacrifices,
holy and pleasing to God—
which is your spiritual worship.
(Romans 12:1)

Chapter 3
Discovering the Essence

❧

God preserved us in important ways during our winter of disfranchisement. He took us to His Word, and He brought friends to our side. Our principal life preserver, however, to which this chapter is devoted, affected me profoundly.

For a number of years prior to this crisis, God was graciously at work, opening my eyes to life's most basic, important, all-encompassing feature: worship.

Of course, I wasn't unaware of God's desire for us to worship Him. In addition to numerous instances of men and women worshiping, the Bible is rather direct about it, as the following verses show:

> Do not worship any other god, for the LORD,
>   whose name is Jealous, is a jealous God. (Ex. 34:14)

> But the LORD, who brought you up out of Egypt with mighty power and outstretched arm, is the one you must worship. To him you shall bow down and to him offer sacrifices. (2 Kings 17:36)

> Rather, worship the LORD your God; it is he who will deliver you from the hand of all your enemies. (2 Kings 17:39)

> Ascribe to the LORD the glory due his name; worship the LORD in the splendor of his holiness. (Ps. 29:2)

Come, let us bow down in worship, let us kneel before the LORD our Maker. (Ps. 95:6)

Exalt the LORD our God and worship at his footstool; he is holy. (Ps. 99:5)

Jesus answered, "It is written: 'Worship the Lord your God and serve him only.' " (Luke 4:8)

God is spirit, and his worshipers must worship in spirit and in truth. (John 4:24)

Therefore, I urge you, brothers, in view of God's mercy, to offer your bodies as living sacrifices, holy and pleasing to God—which is your spiritual worship. (Rom. 12:1)

Therefore, since we are receiving a kingdom that cannot be shaken, let us be thankful, and so worship God accept-ably with reverence and awe. (Heb. 12:28)

Worship him who made the heavens, the earth, the sea and the springs of water. (Rev. 14:7)

No, I had no problem recognizing the command to worship. My problem was understanding and obeying.

My awakening may have been much like yours was or will be: vvveeerrry grrrraaadualll. For years—too many years—I was content to let my local church define "worship" for me, accepting worship as practiced by my adult role models.

The word was used almost exclusively to refer to our Sunday morning services, which seemed to mark the *last* day of the week—an afterthought—rather than the first. There was a specific time and a place for worship. It happened on Sundays, it happened from 11:00 A.M. to noon, and it happened in "the sanctuary."

As time passed, I became vaguely uneasy. Surely there had to be more to it than I and my role models understood.

Eventually God's patient and quickening Spirit moved me from a vague and passive acknowledgment of worship to a proactive pilgrimage of discovery. I began to explore worship in the Bible and to mull over the writing of others who were on this same quest long before I was.

The more I understood, the more He challenged and changed my heart. Have you felt Him work this way in your heart, too? The seed He planted and watered within me slowly broke its shell. I became convinced of my spiritual poverty, regardless of how favorably I might compare myself with Christians around me. I recognized my lack of worship.

My tree, though only a sprout, began to grow.

I saw that real worship is much more than a Sunday experience. First as an intellectual acknowledgment and then sinking eighteen inches down into my heart as a deep-seated conviction, I grasped the fact that true worship is a *lifestyle* experience: Worship occurs *throughout* the week in a variety of ways.

So what? Does it make any difference?

For an answer, look at the people around you. Unless you live in a Christian cocoon—and even there you are probably not exempt—you are surrounded by those for whom high times bring hedonism, low times bring languidness, and in-between times bring the blahs. Offend them, and whether they're on a high, a low, or an in-between, out comes profanity.

Now consider David, in the Old Testament. Whether he was on a high, a low, or an in-between, out came psalms! From boyhood to mature adult, it was the same.

While not ignoring his well-chronicled humanity, observe that worship permeated his life and overflowed from his heart, saturating his lifestyle. No wonder God considered him a man after His own heart (Acts 13:22)!

In return, God took this man whose lifestyle of worship separated him from the ordinary, run-of-the-mill lifestyles of those around him and gave him a significant, fulfilling leadership role in His plan for Israel.

What Is Worship?

You may have some questions: What is worship? Is it good for my business? Does it guarantee corporate success? If I worship enough, will God rescue me from this drab job and make me a king like David, or at least a senior vice-president?

If I am a good worshiper, will God bless me with a big house in an affluent neighborhood? How about a BMW? If I worship well, will God make me popular? Will it help me feel good about myself?

Is it culturally relevant? If worship can't be counted like cash, if it can't be seen like sailboats, and if it can't empower my position, who needs it?

Briefly, the answers are: more than you think, maybe, no, not likely, not likely, not likely, not likely, yes, yes, and you do. (My son Byron, who likes discussions that get right to the point, may regard that as his favorite sentence in this entire book.)

Our word *worship* came from the Anglo-Saxon *weorthscipe*, which later became *worthship*. It means "to attribute worth" to an object. When that object is God, however, a simple word like worthship does not nearly encompass all that is involved!

In recognition of this challenge, many have attempted to communicate the meaning and feeling of worship. For example, the sons of Korah express one aspect of worship with this analogy: "As the deer pants for streams of water, so my soul pants for you, O God. My soul thirsts for God, for the living God. When can I go and meet with God?" (Ps. 42:1-2).

Dwight Bradley, in *Leaves from a Spiritual Notebook*, expressed the manifold nature of worship this way (I put his thoughts on separate lines for emphasis):

> For worship is a thirsty land crying out for rain,
> . . . a candle in the act of being kindled,
> . . . a drop in quest of the ocean . . .
> . . . a voice in the night calling for help,
> . . . a soul standing in awe
> before the mystery of the universe, . . .
> It is time flowing into eternity,
> . . . a man climbing the altar stairs to God.[1]

And a personal favorite, from the pen of William Temple (also on separate lines for emphasis):

Worship is the submission of all our nature to God;
 it is the quickening of conscience by His holiness;
 the nourishment of mind with His truth;
 the purifying of imagination by His beauty;
 the opening of the heart to His love;
 the surrender of will to His purpose
 ... and all of this gathered up in adoration,
 the most selfless emotion
 of which our nature is capable
 and therefore the chief remedy
 for that self-centeredness
 which is our original sin
 and the source of all actual sin.[2]

Even the Bible uses more than one word for "worship." In the Old Testament, two prominent Hebrew words are enlightening. *Hishahawah*—"a bowing down"—describes our approach to God: submissive lowliness and deep respect. *Abodoh*—"service"—describes the highest role we can have in our worship of God.

Likewise, words for "worship" in the New Testament are complementary, dealing with our attitude and our action. *Proskuneo*—"to kiss the hand" or "to bow down"—again denotes humble, reverent adoration. This is the term used in Jesus' conversation with the Samaritan woman by the well (John 4:21-24) as He described the sort of worshiper God seeks.

Latreuo—"to serve" or "to render homage"—(Phil. 3:3 for example) is a revealing verb. It does not describe voluntary service; it describes service that has been *purchased*. When God directed Paul to use *latreuo*, He destroyed forever the misconception that when we serve God, we are "doing Him a favor." The truth is that we *owe* Him our worshipful service. We were redeemed from a future in hell by the love of God the Father and the blood of Christ, His Son.

Inner attitude and outer action—this concept opened new horizons in my thinking. And with these new horizons came practical implications. For example, while it might be more convenient to lock worship into a Sunday morning slot and get it over with for the week, it became clear that a one- or two-hour pit stop at church on Sunday could not satisfy all that worship entails. If I wanted to be a true worshiper, I needed to make worship a *lifestyle.*

But how did worship become such a welcome life preserver for me during my winter?

As we will see in the coming chapters, when we allow worship to soak into and nourish our hearts and lifestyles, God is exalted. But we benefit as well: Life takes on an interesting, energizing dynamic unachievable any other way. *This is our design!* We were born to worship; we were created to celebrate our Creator.

In fact, a perusal of Scripture reveals that the key to fulfillment in life is its orientation to worship: To the extent that my life is worship-centered, it will be fulfilling.

The converse is also true: To the extent that my life is non-worship-centered, it will be eccentric. That is, it will be off-centered, deviant from the true center, perverted, abused, misused. That, I guarantee, will produce extreme stress, frustration, and unfulfillment.

And if this be so, we desperately need to improve our worship. But how?

Chapter 4
Living in Style

❦

Lifestyle worship, which lives out the attitude and action inherent in worship, may be seen as having three components. The first of these is love.

Loving

Christ Himself points to love as the means of our Christian distinction:

"A new command I give you: Love one another. As I have loved you, so you must love one another. All men will know that you are my disciples if you love one another" (John 13:34-35).

Paul shows us that love is the measure of our performance effectiveness:

"If I speak in the tongues of men and of angels, but have not love, I am only a resounding gong or a clanging cymbal. If I have the gift of prophecy and can fathom all mysteries and all knowledge, and if I have a faith that can move mountains, but have not love, I am nothing. If I give all I possess to the poor and surrender my body to the flames, but have not love, I gain nothing" (1 Cor. 13:1-3).

Christ identifies love as the remedy for our religious legalism. One day He was approached by a group of Pharisees, themselves the epitome of bondage to religious trappings. As a test question, they asked Him which law was the greatest.

Christ looked at their smugness and probably sensed the watching crowds who were concerned about violating these religious leaders' long to-do and not-to-do lists. He knew the frustration of those who had given up on the religious system in despair. Filled with compassion, Christ quickly cut through the red tape:

> "Love the Lord your God with all your heart and with all your soul and with all your mind." This is the first and greatest commandment.
> And the second is like it: "Love your neighbor as yourself." All the Law and the Prophets hang on these two commandments. (Matt. 22:37-40)

Have you ever felt overwhelmed by a list that became law? Maybe your music teacher supplied it or your tennis coach. Maybe your parents did or your church.

Lists suffocate love. We become so intrigued with technique that we miss the heart of the matter. Love removes our reliance upon lists when love—not lists—inspires and directs our action.

This love is a heart condition. It is an attitude of willful devotion that manifests itself honorably in a variety of situations:

> Love is patient, love is kind. It does not envy, it does not boast, it is not proud. It is not rude, it is not self-seeking, it is not easily angered, it keeps no record of wrongs. Love does not delight in evil but rejoices with the truth. It always protects, always trusts, always hopes, always perseveres. Love never fails (1 Cor. 13:4-8).

If you and I recognize the reality of this truth about love, we will simplify, prioritize, and thereby energize our lives. As we peel away the superficial checklists one by one, we can get to the heart of the matter—and that's what is important to God.

When we love God and the "neighbors" He has given us as He wants us to, the rest of life falls into its place—with or without prefabricated lists.

Serving

A second component of lifestyle worship is service.

Serving Him is the active expression of our love for God. One way to understand lifestyle worship is in terms of systems analysis, where loving may be viewed as the input and serving the output of worship.

Service is the theme of Romans 12, a beautiful and wide-ranging passage of Scripture which contributes significantly to our understanding of lifestyle worship. Romans 12:1 sets the stage for much of the rest of this book:

> . . . I urge you, brothers, in view of God's mercy, to offer your bodies as living sacrifices, holy and pleasing to God—which is your spiritual worship.

Because much will be said of service later, let's move to the third crucial component.

Abiding

Connecting these two aspects of lifestyle worship is a third element: abiding.

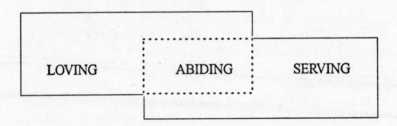

The three components of worship

John 15 compares this "abiding" relationship between our Lord and us to that of a vine and its branches. The branch is designed to bear fruit. However, it can only do so if it remains or abides connected to the vine. It cannot produce the fruit for which it is designed unless it remains connected to the vine. All it has to do is stay connected to the vine and be a conduit. The vine does the rest.

Likewise, our job is to remain connected to the Vine. He will do the rest. We too were designed to bear fruit, to be productive. What fruit? A kind only available through one Source!

Our fruit is the product of God's work in our hearts. Our fruit shows outwardly as enduring qualities of character in ourselves (see 1 Cor. 13:4-8 and Gal. 5:22-23). It also shows in the growth of those same character qualities in others as a result of our service to them in God's name (see Rom. 1:13).

Real branches cannot disconnect themselves from their vine. Unlike branches, however, God created us with the capacity to seek sustenance from other sources than our Vine. We can choose to tie into other popular Vine substitutes, whether a cult, the occult, or another belief system that draws our allegiance away from the God of the Bible.

To do so is to invite personal disaster. We do so against our design (see John 15:5,16 and Eph. 2:10). Instead, we are wise to choose to be nurtured by (remain in) our true Vine . . .

> . . . from whom we draw nourishment, even during
> the winter,
> . . . by whom we are stabilized, even when tossed around,
> . . . to whom we are secondary, no matter what our fans,
> bosses, or employees may say or write about us,
> . . . and for whom we are willing to wait until *His* fruit is
> produced through us not by us.

That is abiding.

It follows, then, that our worshipful abiding allows fulfilling fruitfulness to emerge from our worshipful serving. Fruitfulness is the reason for the branch, the glory of the branch, *but it is also the product of the Vine.*

"Abiding" is part attitude and part action. Our attitude is a willful choice to remain in the true Vine. That is, we choose as Christians to trust the Vine—not some surrogate—to produce the fruit without our attempting to manufacture it independently of Him.

Abiding also has an element of action. Drawing nourishment from Him is an act. Waiting for Him to produce fruit in season is an act. Choosing not to pursue other actions is itself an act. We make a conscious act of faith that He will produce, through us and in His time, fruit that brings glory to His name.

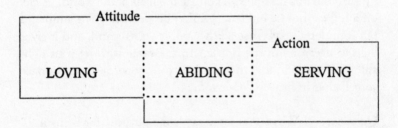

Abiding is part attitude and part action

That's it. Lifestyle worship—loving, abiding, serving—strengthened Jan and me during that difficult winter experience.

Well, what came of it for me? First, my job-loss confronted me with the need to make worship less a Sunday matter and more a Monday-through-Saturday matter. This winter time drove me to deeper growth.

Second, He freed me from a job and ministry that, while enjoyable and worthwhile, was narrower in focus than He designed me to be.

Third, He gave me a completely different career. I could return to California and care for my parents during their time of greatest need. Unbeknownst to me at the time, this new career prepared me for a much more fulfilling role which takes me around the country in public and personal ministry. It enables me also to play a part in God's work around the world. Now isn't it just like God to write such a scenario?

Thanks to Him, that winter passed; spring finally arrived. My tree was still alive, and a time for new beginnings had come.

Synchronizing Agendas

"That's fine for you," you may be thinking. "What about the rest of us trees in the forest? What will happen if we allow true worship to soak into and nourish our hearts and lifestyles?"

One transforming effect is that God's agenda will become your own. What is His agenda? Let's take a brief look at Scripture:

[Jesus told His disciples,] "You are the light of the world. A city on a hill cannot be hidden. Neither do people light a lamp and put it under a bowl. Instead they put it on its stand, and it gives light to everyone in the house. In the same way, let your light shine before men, that they may see your good deeds and praise your Father in heaven." (Matt. 5:14-16)

Question: What does Jesus say is the purpose for being a light in this dark world?

Answer: To cause others to become worshipers of the Most High.

As Jesus talked with the Samaritan woman at the well, He said:

. . . the true worshipers will worship the Father in spirit and truth, for they are the kind of worshipers the Father seeks. (John 4:23)

Question: For whom does He actively search the world? For eloquent preachers? For dynamic evangelists? For popular musicians? For converted addicts and athletes? For jungle-smart missionaries?

Answer: No. His search is much more basic. He wants *real worshipers*—nothing less, no matter how they spend their particular time or earn their living.

Now consider Paul's prayer request for the believers in Rome:

May the God who gives endurance and encouragement give you a spirit of unity among yourselves as you follow Christ

Jesus, so that with one heart and mouth you may glorify the God and Father of our Lord Jesus Christ. (Rom. 15:5-6)

Question: How did Paul, led by the Holy Spirit, view unity among believers?

Answer: He saw unity not as an end in itself, but as a means of expressing an end: undivided worship.

Note that in Paul's letters to the Corinthian and Colossian churches (1 Cor. 10:31; Col. 3:16-17), Paul continues his Spirit-directed theme. We are to treat anything we do—eating, drinking, singing, preaching, teaching, leading, serving—in a way that draws attention and glory to God.

Therein lies the essence of lifestyle worship. What is God's agenda that we will make our own? Worship, plain and simple, permeating and nourishing our hearts. How elegant and un-complicating it is to realize that we the branches are here on earth just to glorify the true Vine.

Wearing Worship Lenses

Okay, so you embrace God's agenda by committing to a lifestyle of worship. What else happens?

As you and I unite in our worship of God, we find our world view profoundly transformed. Does this mean that we walk around day after day, hand in hand, with our heads in the clouds and a faraway look in our eyes? Not likely. No more so than Christ did when He was here on earth.

At certain times we do need to tune out mundane concerns and focus on the Almighty One, as when worshiping in church. Lifestyle worship, however, consists of more than that.

Lifestyle worship means that for most of the week we'll wear "worship lenses." These will give us a new look at those mundane concerns around ourselves, our work and our worlds, which are somewhat different for each of us.

"Worship lenses?" you ask. In Revelation 3:14-18, God told the Laodicean church that they needed eye salve to see themselves and the world as God saw.

Today we use eye lenses to improve our vision, whether contact lenses or otherwise. That's what we need today: worship lenses to filter out the distractions and enhance the features God wants us to observe.

Blossoming Variety

Seeing with God's perspective will generate a burst of variety released in worshipful service. Individually and collectively, we will roll up our sleeves and do what we sense He wants us to do about what we observe around us.

Why the variety? Ministry in and through His church takes teamwork. Effective service requires more capabilities than any one type of person can embody. So while God has given us the privilege of being one body, He has also given us differing, complementary spiritual gifts (see Rom. 12; 1 Cor. 12; Eph. 4; and 1 Peter 4). We activate and develop our different gifts as acts of worship to the Giver.

That in itself breeds variety, but there's more: God has also given us each a number of other "natural" abilities and tendencies. Multiply these gift combinations by those "spiritual" gift combos, and we have unlimited diversity with great potential for adversity as well!

We will find that each of us is sensitive to somewhat different needs and opportunities around us. We will each draw on our own unique group of natural and spiritual gifts as we respond to those needs and opportunities. We will apply these differing resources to address our varying worlds, serving God in differing ways as we unitedly see things as God sees them.

This diversity in our acts of worship provides contrast and balance to the unity in our attitude of worship, just as a well-composed symphony of praise.

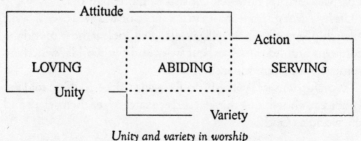

Unity and variety in worship

What is the bottom line? We who perform in this concert will be alike in attitude and different in action. Not only that, we will be pleased to play our complementary parts since they call for us each to operate from strength, to exercise those built-in gifts God gave us. Cellists will play cello, not bassoon. Percussionists will play timpani, not trumpet.

Isn't it just like God, the Master Orchestrator and Conductor, to create such a dynamic symphony? Hallelujah!

Can your life be rescued from the ordinary? Can mine? Can our highs, lows, and in-betweens—especially those repetitive, humdrum in-betweens, where so much of life is lived—be infused with significance?

Yes. And we can also experience two modern-day wonders: a reduction of negative stress and a release of productive energy. How? By embracing a lifestyle of worship that fulfills our design.

For the next several chapters, we will walk thoughtfully down a hallway lined with portraits of various women and men. Behind each portrait is a story. Behind each story is a worshiping heart.

Pondering these very human men and women may help you and me understand God's desire for our unique, significant versions of lifestyle worship.

Chapter 5
Loving Devotedly

❦

"You are worried and upset about many things, but only one thing is needed. Mary has chosen what is better. . ." (Luke 10:41-42).

It's happened to you a thousand times over the years. As the evening of one day gradually settles over the land, you think through tomorrow and plan your schedule. Tomorrow comes, and you make some small changes over breakfast. Then, having planned the work, you begin to work the plan.

Suddenly the phone rings. The call totally reorganizes your day as you deal with the priorities it raises.

Your planned schedule, instead of the navigation chart it was intended to be for the day, becomes just another scrap of paper for your already-overflowing waste basket. The day is transformed from a controlled assault to a frantic scramble.

So it was with Martha. Always in control, she had her list of projects for the day and was busily knocking off one carefully prioritized item after another.

Then word came that Jesus was in town with His disciples. Always the eager hostess, she invited them home for dinner. And "busy" became "frenzied"!

Not to worry though: Martha was in charge. She was seldom happier than when she had a mission and a list: Sweep the porch, stoke the fire, set the table, stir the stew, fetch the water, find some flowers, dust the furniture, wash the feet, change the outfit—and you know someone just like her, right?

Suddenly, while leading an assault on her list, she had the distinctly unpleasant feeling that no one was following her. Mary? Where was Mary? Rushing into the front room from the kitchen, Martha spotted her sister lounging with the guests.

Mary was sitting down. Listening. Watching. Resting. Smiling. Calm. Enraptured. Looking as if she had nothing better to do with her time.

Martha was mad at Mary. And as a child might come to a parent and plead for fairness, Martha burst in on the conversation of her Guest, Jesus of Nazareth. "Lord, don't you care that my sister has left me to do the work by myself? Tell her to help me!"

She had a point. There was a lot left on her "to do" list.

Have you ever seen a child who, though seldom separating the gold-trimmed pages of his or her Bible, will take one look at work that needs to be done around the house and promptly whip out that same Bible for a very spiritual-looking quiet time? Perhaps Martha suspected Mary of using that same work-avoidance tactic.

Not so obvious to most of those present, however, were the hearts behind these behaviors. To Martha's dismay, Christ was not fooled by appearances as she was.

First, He looked into Martha's heart and saw her profound distraction by all her preparations. Second, when He looked into Mary's heart, He saw her active adoration, her unabashed love for God. Wouldn't you like to have heard His conversation with her before—and after—Martha interrupted?

Caring nonetheless for Martha, Jesus turned back to her and spoke the words that begin this chapter: "You are worried and upset about many things, but only one thing is needed. Mary has chosen what is better. . . ."

His brief response, like the sharp scalpel of a skillful surgeon, exposed two infections which had probably festered inside Martha for some time. The first was her misunderstanding and/or intolerance of Mary's "poorly timed" desire to spend a few moments with their Guest.

The second was her own preoccupation with busyness—even the busyness of ministering to the physical needs of the King of kings.

Rebuked, she backed away in confusion and embarrassment.

It's What's Inside That Counts

Let's look at these two women, Mary and Martha, born of the same stock and living in the same house—yet dramatically different in their response to a visit by the King. What happens when we view them through lifestyle worship lenses?

First, lifestyle worship is simple, not complicated. Martha's motivation is not revealed to us as it was to Jesus Christ. Perhaps she was a compulsive perfectionist at heart. Maybe her desire to please the King was based on a need for applause, a desire to hear "well done, good and faithful chef." A very human response.

Whatever her incentive, it led to a long list—and a short fuse. The term translated "distracted" does tell us that she was pulled in different directions by anxious cares. Her competing cares were running her ragged.

And Mary? Mary simply adored Him. Thirstily she sat and drank in every word and move of Jesus Christ. Mary was a living example of Psalm 42:1-2: "As the deer pants for streams of water, so my soul pants for you, O God. My soul thirsts for God, for the living God. When can I go and meet with God?"

The most significant contrast between these two women, then, is not their action but their attention: Martha's was fractured, complicated by competing cares; Mary's was focused, simply centered on the Lord she loved.

Second, lifestyle worship welcomes heart, not formula. Martha was a follower of traditional social customs. People are people, whether of that century or this. Then, as today, it was customary to "knock yourself out" for company. If you didn't, what would they think? What would people say behind your back about your hospitality? Martha was captive to the same syndrome.

Mary followed her heart.

And Christ knew the difference.

Third, lifestyle worship is daring, not dull. Martha was truly distracted, so intent on doing the impressive thing that she missed the real thing.

Jesus perceived this problem immediately and, Friend that He was to her, dared to confront her about her dull conformity, her insensitivity to spiritual reality. "Be different," He challenged her. "Dare to focus on true worship."

Mary, in contrast, dared to do the non-routine. "How can I show Him His worth to me? How can I worthship Him?" Her heart responded, "I've got it! I'll set aside a portion of today's busy schedule and bask in His presence." She made a deliberate decision to withstand the rebuke of her sister, which she probably anticipated, as well as the possible misunderstanding of others in the house that day.

As far as she was concerned, this act of worship would be just a private understanding between her and her Lord. Had she hungered for public notice of her "I love You" to Christ, He would have seen it in her heart and we would likely never have heard of the incident.

Instead, God directed Luke to include it in his account of Christ's life. Consequently, millions of people across hundreds of years have been stirred by the story of Mary.

This anecdote of two sisters could have ended like that of two brothers in Genesis, in which God again showed His approval of one's worship over the other's. When Cain's poorly motivated heart was exposed, he became consumed by bitterness, and in anger he killed his brother.

Not so with Martha. She may have had the proverbial cart before the horse in putting serving ahead of loving, but she was a becomer.

A week before Christ would be crucified, He was back in Bethany for another visit with Martha, Mary, and Lazarus, their brother. Again Martha served dinner, as was the custom. Again Mary broke with tradition . . . as was becoming her custom!

This time, Mary gave Him her most prized possession, a very expensive perfume valued at a year's wages, according to Judas. Not content to simply wrap it up and hand it to Him as a present, she completely used it up anointing His feet. Reverently she poured it over them. Then, in humble adoration, Mary wiped His feet with her hair.

Once more, Mary's unconventional act of loving worship was attacked. This time it was not Martha, but Judas, the disciple/treasurer/thief.

Again Jesus read their hearts and again He rebuked the attacker. Again He affirmed Mary's simple, significant, daring expression of loving worship.

This time Martha said nothing negative about Mary's act, and Jesus said nothing negative about Martha's. Could it be that by this time she had learned how to serve guests without allowing herself to be "drawn in different directions by anxious cares"? Could it be that this time both sisters expressed their love to God in contrasting ways, but with similarly worshiping hearts?

Fourth, lifestyle worship focuses on giving, not receiving. Mary had nothing to gain by incurring Martha's wrath. In a sense she sacrificed a family relationship to feed a spiritual relationship. She jeopardized one to nourish the other.

Her first gift of time and her second gift of treasure came from a heart bent on expressing love, not on seeking special personal favors. More often than we wish to admit, our giving is motivated at least in part by a hoped-for return on that investment. As such, it is impure, unholy.

As Our World Turns

I wonder if there has ever in the history of our species been a time when, individually and collectively, we have been more "drawn in different directions by anxious cares" than right now.

We have the stress of our compulsion to achieve in multiple areas of life at one time. This in itself is enough to shipwreck us.

But there are other forces too. Many worthy charitable and political causes have been organized and marketed to capture your attention: child abuse, battered spouses, drug abuse, cancer, alcohol abuse, heart disease, kidney replacement, teen pregnancy, abortion, euthanasia, neighborhood safety, neighborhood growth control, whales, gun control, oil spills, greenhouse effects, toxic waste, POWs, MIAs, illegal immigrants, homeless people, women's rights, black rights, Indian rights, Hispanic rights. . . .

Sounding almost like an excerpt from the book of Ecclesiastes, every cause under the sun has an organized group to support it. Every group wants your time and your money (but not in that order).

Now, on top of those two backpacks *add* the various activities of your church and other ministry interests: general meetings that someone says you just *have* to attend, smaller group gatherings "which are a *must*" and individuals you need to spend some time with for encouragement, fellowship, or edification.

How often—like Martha—our service *for* Christ crowds out our fellowship *with* Christ. A bit overwhelming, isn't it?

Perhaps *you* are worried and upset about many things, but only one thing is needed. Mary chose what is better; now, why not you?

What should you pursue? What should you eliminate? How can you choose wisely in your life? How can you keep the horse before the cart, loving and abiding before service?

The term "tough love" has caught on in recent years. It refers to our need, at times, to make tough decisions for the sake of those we love.

First Corinthians 13 makes it very clear that unless our interaction with others is permeated with *agape* love, it is a useless waste of time (tautology intended). It does not matter what others may say of it, God knows because He sees our hearts. Before service must come love.

That being true, tough love may call on you and me, as an expression of our love for God, to make some tough choices in our use of time (Mary's first sacrifice) or treasure (Mary's second).

How does a person begin? Do what basketball coaches do when the game is getting out of control: Call a time-out. Get alone with God for a while, calm your racing heart and think "long thoughts," long-range ruminations. You needn't develop a complex plan. Just ask Him what simple ways you might use to show Him how much you love Him. If you mean it, He'll take care of the rest.

Just down the hallway is the portrait of another young woman. Ahhh, she's lovely! But there's a look in her eyes and a set to her chin that hint of grief behind the grace. This person has depth. . . .

Chapter 6
Abiding Resolutely

❦

She had cause to be bitter: She was barren.

Not so, her husband. He had the joy of several children from another marriage. This childlessness was clearly her fault, not his.

Fortunately for him perhaps, but unfortunately for her, his children and their mother lived nearby. The close proximity of these two rivals brought them into constant contact with each other.

Understandably, these contacts were unpleasant. The noxiousness of their relationship was further intensified by their mutual acknowledgment that one of them had several children while the other had a devoted husband. Each felt incomplete without what the other had.

The woman with children lost no opportunity to antagonize the childless wife. Perhaps only another wife who has also been denied motherhood can appreciate the anguish a vicious malcontent can inflict with verbal barbs, condescending innuendoes, and disparaging looks.

It may seem unusual, but both women got together with the extended family on special days of the year. This forced them to be near each other also.

These holidays, of course, were particularly difficult for the childless young wife. The mother had no mercy, taking delight at these family gatherings in driving the non-mother to tears and upsetting her until she could not even eat.

Year after year, this same sad scene was replayed. For the non-mom, it was a wrenching experience.

Have you ever wondered why God allows these things to happen to good people—while He seems to let people with repugnant morals and rancid character have everything they want?

The plot thickens. In 1 Samuel chapter 1, we discover that the man involved in this tragic triangle was named Elkanah. (Elkanah means "whom God possessed"—a refreshing contrast of plot to today's obsession in print and film with possession by demons.)

Why a man whom God possessed would choose to have two wives at one time is a puzzle. It was not one of his smarter decisions. However, such an arrangement was culturally accepted at that time and place. In spite of its legal permissibility, though, the relationship of these two women demonstrates amply that people are people no matter what the century, and putting two women like that together is like combining a delicious banquet with a sensational roller coaster ride: They simply do not mix!

The spouse with children was Peninnah, meaning "coral." Coral is beautiful, but very abrasive. As the account makes clear, Peninnah was true to the dark side of her name in that she was as abrasive to Hannah ("gracious") as coral rock is to tender flesh.

When the Going Gets Tough ...

In those days, men were known by their heritage ("the son of . . . . the son of . . . ," etc.). Women, in contrast, were known by the children, especially sons, they bore; they were known by their production.

Any of us who have been in such areas of business as sales or manufacturing know how it feels to be measured by our production: It's great if we are producing well—and awful if we are behind.

Well, in this situation Hannah felt awful. Peninnah, her rival, was producing. Hannah was not. No matter what she tried, she did not become pregnant. It was not lack of desire, it was not lack of effort, it was not lack of opportunity, and it was not lack of technique. It was, simply, lack of results. God had closed her womb.

Elkanah was a faithful worshiper. Year after year he went to Shiloh as commanded for what was probably the Feast of Tabernacles.

This festival was analogous to our Thanksgiving Day. It was a time to celebrate the memory of God's care during the desert journey to Canaan and a time to thank Him for His blessing on the year's crops. That, of course, heightened Hannah's anxiety: God was withholding His blessing, giving her no "crops." She was barren, unproductive.

There is something in verse 3 that contributes significantly to the story: Note that God is called "the LORD Almighty." It is the first time in the Bible that this term is used! Sometimes translated "the LORD of hosts," this term draws attention to the fact that God is sovereign over all powers in the universe. He is sovereign over human armies, over angelic armies, over evil powers, over the sun and rain which nourish crops—and He is sovereign over the processes that allow a wife to become a mother.

What a dramatic moment to introduce this name for God into Scripture! Here's Hannah, knowing well what Peninnah will do, resolved to worship God with the family anyway, traveling to Shiloh to celebrate her sovereign God's blessing on the crops of other people. She came to worship Him as the LORD Almighty, the One Who could bless her with "crops" too, if He so desired.

Why didn't He want to? Did He enjoy her humiliation every time someone came to these family gatherings with a new child of their own, slyly checking out Hannah's figure or asking subtle little questions to find out if she was pregnant? Why did He allow Peninnah to be such a bitter and malicious rival, to brazenly take advantage of Hannah's vulnerability and anguish, to scrape fiendishly at Hannah's raw wounds?

In her desire to hurt Hannah, Peninnah, noting that Hannah was a woman of worship, perversely selected special worship events as times for special provocation. Part of the worship experience during the Feast of Tabernacles was a thanksgiving dinner which signified fellowship and communion with God. It was this dinner, time after time, that Peninnah took delight in ruining for Hannah.

Have you noticed that family holiday gatherings are often times of high stress? There is the stress of changed schedules and the stress of extra activities. Extra adrenaline flows as you anticipate seeing family members again.

When you finally do get together with them, other stresses creep in. Someone else's career is going better than yours. You may have the uncomfortable feeling that you didn't do or become what you and your relatives had expected in the glory days of your youth. Now you face them and wonder what they really think of you behind their happy face masks.

Maybe they are very married and you are still single. Or their spouse is better-looking than yours. Someone else got a new car, a new house, or a new baby.

"God, why me? Is this what I get for worshiping You? Did I do something wrong? Are You listening when I cry for help? Why did You not only close my womb, but also open my rival's? Is there no justice? Is it that You just don't care?"

On a scale from one to ten for self-worth, Hannah probably registered a minus-nine. Rejected. Set aside. Shattered. Desolate. And very desperate.

What happens to a person who is that stressed, that shattered, that defeated, that desperate? And have you ever felt that way?

Hurt. Confusion. Anger. Then bitterness. Yes, Hannah became bitter; bitter about her unending unproductiveness and about the painful attacks of her relentless rival.

If you have ever been bitten by bitterness, you know its insidiousness. It's like toxic waste in one's emotional system.

It clouds one's perception, as we see happening to Hannah in verse 8. In her bitterness and confusion, she overlooked her greatest blessing and the very reason Peninnah was being such a jealous pain: Hannah had a husband who loved her deeply.

Absorbed by this or that pressure, many times I too have ignored the blessings God showered on me. Haven't you? We do understand Hannah, don't we? How easily we are contaminated; how readily we succumb.

At such a time, we need an anchor and a harbor. We need a certain kind of friend and a quiet place to rest.

This is a time when *abiding* becomes essential.

Hannah had an anchor and a harbor. Her anchor was the LORD Almighty, and her harbor was His temple. In spite of her hurt, her confusion and her bitterness, she knew where to go for refuge. She resolved to remain with Him. She determined to "abide," to wait on Him.

Excusing herself from dinner, she escaped to her harbor, the temple. Once inside, she poured out her heart to the One she loved. Again we see the significance of her choice of words: She cried out to God with the name emphasizing His unqualified sovereignty, "the LORD Almighty."

"Give me a son," she bargained, "and I will give him back to You for life."

Again we understand Hannah, don't we? How often we have bargained. "God, if You will just get me out of this jam; just let me achieve that goal; just let me be rich; just let me marry him (or her); just give me success in this venture, I'll live wholeheartedly for You the rest of my life."

In spite of us, He is a wonderful and merciful God. The LORD Almighty did hear Hannah's cry and answer her affirmatively. Through Eli the priest, He assured her that she would bear a son.

It was winter now, but spring was coming. The barren tree was about to blossom.

What a Difference a Prayer Makes . . .

And now, as Paul Harvey would say, you know the rest of the story . . . of the birth of the prophet Samuel. His mother did bring him to the temple, committing him to a lifetime of ministry as she had vowed.

There, the son she almost never bore became one of the most influential people in Old Testament history. As judge, prophet, king-maker and king-breaker, Samuel cut a wide swath.

God continued to bless Hannah, giving her several more children. Her former rival, Peninnah, is not mentioned later in Scripture, to be remembered only as the abrasive and heartless antagonist of the future mother of Samuel. What a memorial.

Hannah, in contrast, is immortalized in Scripture as a person characterized by lifestyle worship. She became a testimony and encouragement to all ages by keeping her trust in God and keeping her vow to God. Her acts of worship, as we have seen earlier, were simple but not easy, whole-hearted, daring, ongoing, sacrificial. What a glory to God!

Branching Out from There

How will people reminisce about you and me? The implications for us are profound.

The Gospel of John, chapter 15, uses an analogy of the Vine (Jesus Christ) and its branches (us) to focus on the importance of practicing the worship of abiding.

To abide or remain in the Vine means that we stay connected to Him; we do not search elsewhere for that which He alone can provide. As branches, we draw nourishment from that Vine. We are identified with that Vine. We are secondary to that Vine. We are stabilized by that Vine.

Inherent in the worship of abiding, as Hannah discovered, is a dynamic, uncomfortable parenthetic period. It is called *the worship of waiting.*

Abiding asks us to play a humble but crucial role *after* we have poured out our heart to God regarding a particular concern. During this parenthesis, this interruption of continuity, we wait for His response to our request. We wait for His fruit to be produced in us. We wait for His work to be accomplished around and through us. We wait for His name to be glorified.

I have described in the first couple of chapters one of my most significant parentheses. I'm certain that you have had yours too.

Waiting is a very un-American idea. "I'll get back to you right away." "We'll send it out in today's mail." "Quick as a wink, away goes the stink." "Breakfast in ten minutes, or it's free." "Don't keep the customer waiting." "Can you fax it to me?" The very term *wait* suggests to us the unflattering thought that we are less important than someone or something else.

God has a different view and a different set of priorities for us. He looks beneath the immediate crisis and checks our character to see how we are growing. In His time, usually different from ours, He answers. Our inner life is more important to Him than our outer circumstances. Our priorities are usually the reverse.

Waiting can be beautiful. The psalmist says, "Be still, and know that I am God" (Ps. 46:10). His command is to cease striving, to relax, to let go. He is God, and He can handle it—whatever "it" may be. As Hannah let go of her burden and bitterness in the temple, so must we.

Waiting may still be a time of action. When my job was taken from me, I needed to couple faith with works, as James exhorts us. I had to combine looking to God with looking for employment. The worship of waiting does not free us from action so much as it frees us from anxiety.

Waiting can also be renewing. Isaiah wrote, "Those who hope in [wait for] the LORD will renew their strength" (Isa. 40:31).

The idea of hoping or waiting is that of entwining one's heart with the Lord's. That takes time, but what a profoundly wonderful experience that is for us.

And the result? Our strength is renewed, nourished, exchanged for His.

Waiting may be for a short time, a long time, or a lifetime on earth. It is His time that counts. We are His workmanship, His work of art, and we dare not rush the Master.

From the portrait of Mary, we learned God's priority of love. This portrait of Hannah reveals her resolve to abide in His love: "As the Father has loved me, so have I loved you. Now remain in my love" (John 15:9).

A few more steps down the hallway bring us to the portrait of a short, balding man with close-set eyes, crooked legs, and a slightly hooked nose. Note, however, his vigorous physique. He's a man whose life story would make Indiana Jones sit up and take notes.

He, of all people, is qualified to discuss what Americans find to be the most attractive aspect of the lifestyle worship trilogy. He wrote the book on this subject.

I think, if we just press this button underneath the picture, that we can get in on an interview. . . .

Chapter 7
Serving Effectively

❧

Sure enough, the button turns on a taped interview, from which the following is transcribed:

Interviewer (I): Pictured here is one of the most influential figures in the body of Christ. It is my privilege to be able to ask him some questions about his life and work. Saul—er, Paul—first of all, which name would you prefer that we use to address you?

Paul (P): "Paul" is fine.

I: Originally, your name was Saul. Why did you change? Is Paul a stage name?

P: To answer your second question first, yes—sort of. Much as a stage name connotes a different identity, my new name reflects the fact that I am a different person from who I was earlier. In a sense, I am a new creation.

I: I see. So you are into reincarnation?

P: No, but I'm glad you asked. This body is the same one I used to have, it's the only one, as we know them, that I will ever have, and it's wearing out rather quickly—I've put a lot of kilometers on it in a very short time.

I: *So what is new?*

P: A part of me you cannot see. God is in my heart, and I am in Christ through faith in Him and commitment to Him. He radically changed my life, He made old things pass away—although I still do battle with the world, the flesh, and the devil—and all things become new. He renewed my mind, transforming my perspective about everything that has to do with this world and life hereafter.

I: *Paul, your encounter with Christ was dramatic. As you reflect on that experience, what thoughts come to mind?*

P: Well, the details of that event are well documented in Acts, a book written by my personal friend and physician, Luke.

However, taking a step back and looking at the broader picture, I'd have to say that God dealt with me as my personality required.

I have always been a fairly focused, energetic, determined person. When I decide what I need to do, I ignore everything else and zero in on it, and it gets done—well done, in fact. I'm an achiever, and woe to the person who gets in my way when I'm busy achieving.

I was in that mode while on my way to Damascus in pursuit of Christians, whom I then considered to be the rogues of the religious world. I was intent on hunting them down and crushing them permanently for the havoc they created for the religious system I espoused.

Given that mind-set, God did what He needed to do to get my attention. And believe me, He got it!

I: *And promptly after your encounter with Jesus Christ came a flurry of seminars in every major city, the publication of several books, and a burst of successful church plants. Royalties rolled into your pockets and royalty rolled out their red carpets. You had a house in every country and two chariots in every courtyard. . . .*

P: Stop! Your last comment has more pus than pith. It reeks of infected thinking. If I hadn't caught the twinkle in your eyes, I'd be seething beneath my outer calm and debonair demeanor.

I: *You're right; it was just jest. Can I assume, then, that you are not a disciple of prosperity theology?*

P: I am a disciple of Jesus Christ, who loves us so much that He—although in very nature God—did not grasp for the status and privileges to which He was entitled as God, but made Himself nothing, laying aside the glory and high position of deity and taking the form of a servant to the extent that He was even crucified on a wooden cross like a common crook.

His example, my friend, directs His disciples 180 degrees away from the lifestyle trumpeted by the prosperity preachers who parade around their circuit—or is it their circus?

Waiting in the Wings

I: *What happened, then, following your conversion?*

P: Except for two brief, life-threatening ministry episodes, I essentially experienced about ten years of obscurity, and not by personal choice, I must confess.

Once I understood how wrong I had been in opposing Jesus Christ, I was more determined to be about my Savior's business than I had been earlier to destroy it.

However, I still had much to learn about Him before I was truly prepared to serve Him as effectively as He intended. That learning curve required that I be benched for a while—quite a while.

I: *Tell us more about that time in your life. Some of us fear we've been benched by God, too. Maybe you can help us gain insight regarding our situations.*

P: First of all, God treats all of us alike with regard to the fact of our need for the salvation which comes only through His Son, Jesus Christ.

Second, beyond that He is incredibly creative in working out the details of the lives of each of His individual children. No two are exactly alike.

In my case, several years of obscurity were spent alone out in the Arabian desert—stage one of my parenthesis period. After truncated visits to Damascus and Jerusalem, several more years of obscurity—stage two—were spent back home, deep in the heart of Tarsus.

He used those years of obscurity to slow me down, ease the pounding of my heart, quiet my mind, and reveal Himself to me in a way that I simply cannot put into words. I learned more of His law, more of His love, and more of His grace than ever before or since.

As a result, I found myself *loving* Him more and more. I also learned to rest in Him, to remain in Him, to *abide* in Him in a way that I doubt could have happened had I not been on the sidelines. It was quite a time of worship.

Please understand, however, that I was not totally idle. God used me to help and encourage individuals from time to time in my home town as I resumed my tentmaking activities. Let me tell you, I was thrilled to have even a small part in building up their faith after all I had done to destroy it earlier!

Yet, I longed for the opportunity to serve Him on a wider scale. I yearned to be out on the field, in the center of the action.

This was not blind ambition. Nor was it a personal desire for greatness; I had already humbled myself irrevocably by my pre-conversion actions. This was a God-implanted desire to invest myself in the building of His church across the continent.

I wanted, in serving God, to serve hundreds—maybe thousands—of other believers. But I didn't know when—or if—it would happen.

All I knew for sure was that I loved Him, that I needed to abide in Him and to be faithful in what few things He gave me to do until or unless He led me otherwise. It was a time to work, to watch, and to wait for His move.

I: Were there any particular obstacles facing you during those years of obscurity?

P: Yes. My ever-active mind kept replaying my leading role as an antagonizer of those who loved Jesus and knew Him as the Christ. Satan clubbed me time after time with vivid memories of the faces of believers I imprisoned, of families I split, and of Stephen, in whose murder I participated.

Sometimes in the middle of the night and other times in the heat of day, I would be jolted by flashbacks: husbands I snatched from their wives, mothers I separated from their babies, children whose parents I had just put into chains and paraded down the street in a public spectacle.

Their eyes haunted me. I felt their tug on my clothes. I heard their anguished voices begging for mercy.

These memories tormented me. I became the one begging for mercy. Repeatedly I cried out, "What a wretched man I am! Who will rescue me?"

I: *And how were you rescued?*

P: God rescued me. First, He took me under His wing and nourished our relationship. He forgave me, an experience that felt like cool rain on parched ground. He assured me of His unchanging love. He convinced me that I belonged to Him.

Second, He took me to His Word, reminding me of such leaders as Moses and David, who each experienced a significant delay between the time of their calling to crucial service and their engagement in that service.

Third, He brought people to my side as encouragers. Ananias and Barnabas each played particularly important roles in braving the elements to come beside me and help.

Serving Center Stage

I: *Would you care to comment on the years following your paren-thesis period?*

P: Well, as I wrote in my letter to the believers in Rome, the reasonable thing to do when confronted with God's love and all He has done is offer oneself—body, mind, everything—to Him and become a loving and devoted servant. There is no logical alterna-tive. It is a tangible, exciting form of worship!

I gave myself primarily to spreading the gospel to the Gentiles. I traveled extensively, speaking in synagogues and establishing churches in a variety of cities. Other ministry opportunities also emerged as I went about my Father's work.

I: How did you choose that particular context of service?

P: From the time of my conversion, God made clear to me that He wanted me to spread His Gospel to the Gentiles. God even told Ananias, the first believer I encountered, that I was to reach out to the non-Jewish world, so it would have been difficult not to recognize what He intended for me—even though I did not yet know the details of His plan.

I realize that not everyone receives so clear a calling to a specific ministry, but it underscores again the fact that He deals with each of us individually. We dare not box Him in by telling Him how He should inform us of what He wants us to do!

In addition to the calling, God equipped me for this task. He gifted me as a leader, an exhorter, a preacher, and teacher. He gave me high energy and made me a self-starter. He gave me no family responsibilities, leaving me free to focus fully on my work. These and other factors assured me that I was custom-designed for this ministry.

In fact, every believer is custom-designed for the ministry God intends that person to have.

I: And as you moved forward with this assurance, God gave you uninterrupted success, right?

P: I see that twinkle again! The answer is no, if you mean success as our world system thinks of it. There were discouraging setbacks in the churches I helped plant. There were also tension-filled disagreements within the ranks.

One argument I will never forget was between Barnabas, my dear friend and encourager, and myself regarding John Mark. We had taken this young man on an earlier trip, but he had deserted us before we finished. I can't stand quitters, and yet Barnabas wanted to encumber us with him again.

I: What happened next?

P: Our conflict of opinion became explosive, and it split us up. Barnabas took Mark on his missionary trip, and I took Silas on mine.

I: *That sounds like a ministry setback.*

P: That's how it felt, too. Actually, however, God used that paroxysm to help spread the work and the Word. It amazes me how creative the Master Craftsman is with clay, cracked pots like us!

I: *So there were setbacks in churches you helped and setbacks in relationships you had. Anything else?*

P: You don't quit either, do you! Yes, there were also setbacks in my physical condition. I was chased, imprisoned, whipped, stoned, left for dead, shipwrecked, and afflicted continuously with a malady from which there was no relief.

I: *Well, that about does it for the idea that a dedicated Christian has the inside track on health, wealth, and popularity. Why did you put up with all that? Weren't you ever tempted to retreat into the safety and comfort of making tents and being nice to your neighbors?*

P: On a human level, remember that I'm a finisher. When my body wants to quit, my mind says, *don't even think about it!*

On a much higher level, one that transcends personality or grit, we all need to think beyond the moment. Life on earth is as brief as a blink, compared with the everlasting timelessness of eternity. We all need to redeem our time by giving God the worship of service.

We may not bear the same scars of God's service on our bodies, but we must bear the same marks of His love on our hearts.

Furthermore, our present sufferings are not worth comparing with the glory that will be revealed in us. We are heirs of God and co-heirs with Christ, and sharing in His sufferings—whatever form that sacrifice may take—is dwarfed in comparison with the glory we will also share with Him in the future.

I: *As we bring this much-appreciated conversation to a close, Paul, are there some guidelines for every believer to keep in mind as he or she ponders ways of expressing the worship of serving?*

P: Yes. Although the worship of serving may be expressed in a thousand different ways, those manifestations are the outgrowth of some vital constants. Let me recapitulate a portion of my letter to the Roman church which addresses your question.

For each of us, life consists of our private world and our public world. Let's touch the private world first.

Your private world encompasses what happens inside you. Step one is crucial: If you want Jesus Christ to be Lord of *every* area of your life, you will commit yourself to become a living sacrifice to Him.

No more substitutions, as was the practice in the days of temple worship. You offer yourself—your entire self—to God.

When you yield your mind to Him as part of that sacrifice, He renews it like foliage in the spring. The result is a metamorphosis, created in you by God, which will make you significantly different from those who accept the world's pattern of priorities and practices.

But I must remark that it is a bit misleading to call this process a sacrifice, since by "sacrificing" yourself you gain and by retaining yourself you lose.

Back to my main point, this misperceived "abnormality" is actually a *normal* effect of your worship of loving and your worship of abiding.

Incidentally, if you want to study an excellent example of such nonconformity, look at the life of Jehoshaphat. What a guy! He was a dramatic and godly man.

Added to this commitment and this transformation in your private world is a third component: a sober, realistic view of yourself. You need a sane, wise estimate of the capabilities God has given you. This is how you discover your customized design!

Your public world encompasses your relationships with those around you. Are you joyfully and diligently using the gifts and abilities God gave you?

Are you loving others sincerely, rather than simply playing the game? Are you eager to honor others above yourself? Are you hard-working?

These and other questions reveal the many ways we serve as an act of worship. It goes deeper than what we do; it is also how we do it and why.

When we serve in worship, God makes our service effective. The fruit is His work; we are just the branches.

I: *Thank you, Paul, for living what you preached.*

P: To the only wise God be glory forever through Jesus Christ!

I: *Amen.*

Woven into the last several chapters are five features of lifestyle worship. While these characteristics may be constant, their expression through different individuals creates a remarkable and beautiful contrast.

Having stretched higher to embrace what God has for us, let's note these distinctions now as we shift our attention to an inward look at ourselves.

PART 3:
LOOKING INWARD

Do not conform any longer
    to the pattern of this world,
but be transformed
    by the renewing of your mind. . . .
Do not think of yourself more highly
    than you ought,
    but rather think of yourself with
    sober judgment. . . .
    (Romans 12:2-3)

Chapter 8

Facing Up to Expectations

❧

Alfred North Whitehead had an interesting and thought-provoking perspective on worship:"The worship of God is not a rule of safety—it is an adventure of the spirit . . . ."[3]

For almost a decade, I have had the privilege and responsibility of helping people in their long-range financial planning. Occasionally individuals claim to want their investments to out-pace inflation—yet they cling to investment tools characterized by maximum safety of principal and, generally, low return. Clearly, their priority is safety, not growth.

Sometimes a baseball analogy helps them understand the dynamics of their decision-making: You can't get to second base unless you take your foot off of first!

The same analogy applies to true worship. Making Romans 12 the story of your life can take you out to the margins of comfortableness.

King David, in 2 Samuel 6, certainly had a different perspective on worship than did his wife Michal! This is the occasion he danced before God and Israel "with all his might"—and without his royal robes—as the Ark of the Lord was being carried into the City of David. Michal met his act of worship with utter contempt and disdain. One person's "adventure of the spirit" may be another's dismay!

In the past several chapters, we sensed the adventures of worship experienced by these spiritual kinsmen. Before we examine others, however, let's look at several common threads connecting these contrasting acts of worship. This chapter focuses on the first of five features which help us understand lifestyle worship.

Distinction #1: Lifestyle worship is simple, not complicated.

Mary simply stopped rushing, sat down, and listened at His feet. Hannah simply refused revenge, knelt down, and worshiped in His temple. Paul simply fought the good fight, finished the race, and kept His faith.

Lifestyle worship is simply the heart expressing itself in life. A healthy Christian daily seeks to follow Christ's example. As His life expressed worship, so should ours. Think of it as the word *Christian* is spelled: It is "I" following "Christ."

Our agenda is simple: to embody meaningful Christian living. That is, our lifestyles must be characterized by observable expressions of our worship of God. (Observable need not suggest well-publicized, by the way.)

Christians live as forgiven and adopted children of God in a corrupted world system. We are pilgrims. While we belong on the planet Earth temporarily, our permanent citizenship is in heaven.

Some of the cultural norms around us do not fit us. They reflect one master; we have Another. It comes as no surprise, then, that at times our behavior will not conform to the societal norms of others near whom we live or work.

"If," you ask, "our agenda is to embody meaningful Christian living, then is there also such a thing as meaningless or insignificant Christian living?" As we look around and within, we must acknowledge, yes.

At times we follow Christ distantly, as Peter did just prior to Christ's crucifixion. Bolstered by a sympathetic group, in church meetings for example, we may mouth the right words and make the right moves.

However, sometimes our worship wanes and we melt into the crowd while in hostile territory, such as the Monday marketplace. At those times we each provide our personalized example of meaninglessness, of eternal insignificance, no matter how much resulting money we make or power we wield.

Peer pressure? Social facilitation? Give it any label you wish, but it still looks a lot like compromise.

There's not a Christian alive who hasn't compromised many times along his or her daily pilgrimage. That's what sin is all about, and our confession. And His forgiveness.

However, some seem to be characterized by this distant following. Are they true Christians, albeit sickly? Only God knows, and it's His opinion that counts. At best, they are team members who are not contributing to, and may even be undermining, the team effort.

'Tis a Gift to Be Simple

Again, lifestyle worship is *simple*. Simple is not the same as *easy*. Nowhere in the Bible does God say worship is easy. We've got the world, our flesh, and the devil against us. Any of the three alone would be quite enough to provide us with challenging difficulties, but the truth is that there may be times when we are tested by all three at once.

The good news is this: Against that tireless and tricky trinity we have the Trinity before whom all else pales. We have God the Father, God the Son, and God the Holy Spirit!

Therefore, as we walk onward in our pilgrimage we can acknowledge our spiritual enemies without cowering. We can move forward with Christ in our hearts, His name on our lips, and His blood as our power.

We may lose skirmishes, but the victory has already been won by Christ and—think of it!—He has allowed us the inestimable privilege of being on His team. Praise God, from whom all blessings flow!

Well, so much for "easy." How about "simple"?

We tend to make simple things complicated. Who knows why? Maybe we just like the challenge. Maybe we subconsciously think that something has to be complicated before it is worthy of our esteemed attention. Regardless of the reasons, we tend to make simple things complicated.

From time to time as I grew up, I would try this or that "shortcut" to get whatever I was doing finished quicker or better. Many of my shortcuts didn't work, of course, and I remember my dad kidding me more than once with, "If there's a difficult way to do this, you'll find it!"

Our lives can easily become cluttered with complicating and encumbering shortcuts. For quick money, we fall for get-rich-fast schemes or take on multiple jobs. For quick advancement, we jam-pack our schedules with activity designed to impress our bosses. For quick spiritual growth, we read a five-minute devotional.

Satan must laugh in derision at our gullibility for such tactics. He probably thrives on our worry and impatience.

One simplifying step you and I can take toward a lifestyle of worship, therefore, is to examine ourselves for pseudo-shortcuts. What are they? Why are they there?

As we then release our concerns to Him as an expression of our loving and abiding in Him, He will produce on our branches the fruit of His Spirit: peace and patience. That in turn will sanctify, or set apart, our service to Him.

So, What Did You Expect?

There is another way we can complicate our entire lives and compromise our effectiveness: by burdening ourselves with unrealistic expectations that are either too high, too low, too wide, too narrow, or too distracting, taking us away from the heart of our design.

Some of these are self-imposed. For example, we take something at which we're fairly good, work or play, and spoil our fun by flogging ourselves for not doing it to perfection. What a relief it is when we mature to the point where, instead of focusing on our flaws, we simply try to be better at our performance! Our process is then much more affirming and our product probably much more pleasing.

Too High

Too Narrow

Off-track

Too Wide

Too Low

Examining our unrealistic expectations

Tennis is one of my favorite pastimes. It gives me lots of action, an opportunity for casual social contact, and a form of health insurance. But it also reveals my lower nature! There are times, as my tennis colleagues will confirm, that I erupt in Romans 7-type anguish at myself over another sloppy shot brought on by another lapse in thought. Those frustrations are cogent personal reminders of self-imposed expectations that may be too high for my level of practice or training.

Added to our unreasonable demands on ourselves are the burdens we let significant others place on our shoulders: their expectations of us. Do you remember the Pharisees? They had their followers hog-tied with how-to-do-its. Their rules were too high, too narrow, *and* off-track.

Their rules ruined people's lives. Those who honestly decided they wouldn't continue the charade quit in bitterness, burdened with a sense of failure. Not unlike many who today have left our legalistic churches, I suppose.

Others who sincerely loved God tried to keep jumping through the Pharisee-designed hoops like obedient slaves. They were seemingly unaware of the freedom of true worship.

Around you, and perhaps within you, is an adult person still trying desperately—even if subconsciously—to please a "significant other." A daughter still struggles for an "I'm proud of you!" from the mother who voiced such great expectations of her as a child.

A pastor with fifteen years of ministry experience is still, in the back of his mind, preaching to his homiletics professor's expectations instead of his congregation's needs. An attorney, unhappy and unfulfilled in her career, is still plugging away at it because her father expected her to come into the family practice.

A particular tragedy occurs when the expectations point in one direction while the person's potential points in another, as with the attorney mentioned above. Once again, we complicate God's mix by adding our own ingredients. The result is a mediocre, diminished life.

Another step toward your lifestyle of worship, then, is facing up to expectations in your life. What have you imposed on yourself: Perfection? Forget it. Accept what everyone else already knows: You're flawed, friend. Supermom status? There's a national organization, Supermoms Anonymous, dedicated to burned out victims of your genre. Superdad? Super-salesman? Super-church-activist? My condolences. You'd better hope someone sticks around you to pick up the pieces.

Whose list of expectations are you trying to fulfill in addition to your own? Your elderly parents'? Your former teacher's? Your self-serving child's? Your ambitious spouse's? Madison Avenue's? Things get rather tangled up, don't they?

God's advice to us comes as sunshine to the bitter cold, as spring to the brutal winter: love, abide, serve.

Were we the faithful lovers God desires, our schedules would be pruned much more discerningly. Were we the faithful lovers God desires, our ministry to others would blossom much more fruitfully. Were we the faithful lovers God desires, our lives would be lived much more fulfillingly.

The question posed by the sixties singing group Peter, Paul, and Mary comes back to haunt us: When will we ever learn? When will we ever learn?

Simplicity, distinction #1 of lifestyle worship, is a call to untangle ourselves from things in our current lifestyle which bind us. It is a call to reexamine and relieve ourselves of worshipless expectations which burden us.

❧

Mary, Hannah, Paul, and others exemplify several other features which combine to help distinguish lifestyle worshipers from the rest of the pack. Let's see what they are, in the next chapter.

Chapter 9
Getting Back to Basics

The previous chapter took a look at the first of five features of lifestyle worship: Lifestyle worship is simple, not complicated. As we continue in this chapter, the remaining features will be more succinct, but just as important.

Distinction #2: Lifestyle worship welcomes heart, not formula.

Mary's loving, Hannah's abiding, and Paul's serving show no sign of time-encrusted ritual. Their brand of worship was a gut-level, a heart-level conviction of what to do—for which no formulas were developed!

In Genesis 4:2-5 God recounts the story of two offerings made to Him by the sons of Adam and Eve. Cain, the farmer in the family, "brought some of the fruits of the soil" to God. Abel, the rancher in the family, "brought fat portions from some of the firstborn of his flock" to the Lord as a sacrifice.

God responded to Abel's sacrifice with favor, but the offering of Cain received no such regard. Why not? Was it because Abel offered animal life, whereas Cain offered plant life?

The author of the epistle to the Hebrews points to the distinction: "By faith Abel offered God a better sacrifice than Cain did. By faith he was commended as a righteous man, when God spoke well of his offerings" (Heb. 11:4).

The significant difference was not in the formula, but in the heart. Cain observed the formality of making an offering, but he did so without faith. His offering, naturally then, was devoid of thought, devoid of care, and devoid of heart. He simply complied because it was expected; he did it because it looked good to his family. His expression to God thereby was of his *lack* of worship.

God reacted in kind, spitting it out and rebuking Cain, "This is lukewarm at best. I don't like it, I don't accept it, and you are headed for trouble unless your heart changes" (Gen. 4:5-7, author's paraphrase).

In contrast, Abel brought generous, choice portions of his ranch to God. Drawing these portions from the firstborn of his flock indicated his recognition that all fruit of the flock comes from the Father; it all belongs to God.

Abel's heart was revealed before God. His offering expressed his worship of the Almighty One. It was his "I love You!" to Jehovah.

And God said, "I love you, too, Abel."

God makes clear what is—and is not—important to Him: "The Lord says: 'These people come near to me with their mouth and honor me with their lips, but their hearts are far from me. Their worship of me is made up only of rules taught by men' " (Isa. 29:13).

Christ echoed this verse during his castigation of the Pharisees (see Matt. 15:8-9), remarking that Isaiah prophesied about them. Could it be that this prophecy applies to our time as well? Are we still making rules—rather than heart condition—the focus of our attention?

Distinction #3: Lifestyle worship is daring, not dull.

The lifestyle we are considering centers on our worship of God. Read again the words of William Temple:

> Worship is the submission of all our nature to God;
> it is the quickening of conscience by His holiness;
> the nourishment of mind with His truth;
> the purifying of imagination by His beauty;
> the opening of the heart to His love;
> the surrender of will to His purpose
> . . . and all of this gathered up in adoration,
> the most selfless emotion

of which our nature is capable
and therefore the chief remedy
for that self-centeredness
which is our original sin
and the source of all actual sin.[4]

True worship is observable. True worship precipitates significant action. Our hearts express themselves in our lives.

Such living leads people into meaningful nonconformity. Until Christ's Second Coming, such people will be in the minority. Undaunted by cultural norms, however, their worshiping hearts will lead them to step out of the ordinary in ways which vary from person to person. After all, by definition, to be significant one must be meaningfully different from the crowd.

When you or I dare to be different in the spirit of Romans 12:2, we may make headlines. This is what God did, for example, with the ministry of the apostle Paul. A contemporary illustration of high profile ministry is that of Dr. James Dobson through Focus on the Family.

Other times, our daring to be different may be a matter of the heart, known only to God. It may involve, for example, our decision to do something we are not inclined to do—or not do something that we desire to do.

Either way, no one is ever likely to know about it. Whether personally mundane or momentous, making that simple decision can be a private expression of worship, a secret "I love You!" to God. Such was the worship of Mary and Hannah. They didn't know their stories would be told for centuries!

Most of the time, our renewed minds will lead to creative nonconformity in the day-to-day process of living. It will show in our ongoing use of time, of money, and of the abilities we received from God for investment during our rather brief pilgrimage on earth.

Distinction #4: Lifestyle worship is a continuing process, not an instant event.

This may seem so obvious that it need not be noted. However, the expectations of most Americans alive today have been profoundly affected by instantaneity. Think of microwave ovens, fast-food restaurants, satellite communications, news sound bytes, fast-paced TV action, incredibly quick computer calculations, and a host of other developments with an emphasis on "hurry."

Given our mind-boggling technological capabilities, does it surprise you that we come subtly to expect our spiritual and mental sides to be "instantly" transformed into Romans 12:2 living?

We pray, "Zap me, Lord. Make me an instant blessing to those around me." Or, "Give me patience, Lord. Now!"

It doesn't have to make sense; we tend to accept such leaps without being particularly concerned about the logic involved or the cost of doing it right.

In Psalm 1, in the life of Joseph, and in the life of David, God trumpets process, process, process. In Paul, we see the process of dogged godliness. The very verb God led Paul to use in Romans 12:2, concerning the "renewing" of our minds, indicates that it is an ongoing process rather than a one-time event.

In Jesus' time on earth, He submitted to the disciplines of process: fellowshiping, fasting, being tested, enduring, praying, working, waiting, sacrificing, suffering, abiding in God.

Like marriage, lifestyle worship is a one-time commitment, but that vow is affirmed time after time in a continuous series of choices and actions of one kind or another. After all, juicy, refreshing fruit does not pop out of a tree branch like an apple out of a vending machine! Instead it emerges slowly and gradually, the product of time, nurture, and winter.

If you and I are to live lives of worship, we must let the process begin. Then we will be wise to be patient. Significant living, we may discover, is closer to a fast than to a hurry.

Distinction #5: *Lifestyle worship focuses on giving, not receiving.*

Paul minces no words: "Therefore, I urge you, brothers, in view of God's mercy, to offer your bodies *as living sacrifices*, holy and pleasing to God—which is your spiritual worship" (Rom. 12:1, emphasis added).

Perhaps the most difficult pill to swallow, especially for Americans, is the thought of giving without obligating a reciprocal benefit from the receiver. We frequently trade favors in business and neighborhood life. We offer help with the implied understanding that that person will do the same for us when we need it. That's not bad, either!

It's just not how lifestyle worship works. With God, if we give in order to get, then we give amiss. We are then thinking of ourselves first and of God second—a dangerous order of priorities.

Lifestyle worship will benefit us, but it is not primarily for our benefit. If our focus is ultimately on ourselves, then we fall into the witless trap of worshiping a compromised creation instead of our incomparable Creator. Such truncated vision will produce personal barrenness.

Lifestyle worship is sacrificial. A sacrifice is a gift of something we value. A living sacrifice is a gift of the essence or the product of our lives. It may be a gift of our time, a gift of our talent, or a gift of our treasure. Whatever shape it takes, it is a sacrifice given with no regard for a return on that investment.

Mary's sacrifice was time. She devoted a portion of this irretrievable commodity to sitting at the feet of Christ instead of spending it on His meal. This, in turn, sacrificed peace in the household as Martha vented her anxiety in the presence of all her guests.

Hannah sacrificed the momentary pleasure of personal revenge on her rival, leaving that instead to God. She also sacrificed her treasure, Samuel, giving him up as a child to full-time, lifetime temple ministry rather than keeping him at home where she could see, care for, and enjoy her son as other moms did their children.

Paul sacrificed health, wealth, marriage, comfort, and prestige in order to devote himself to the mission of bringing the Gospel to the Gentiles of his generation. All of us who are Gentiles today can thank him for his faithfulness to that calling.

The sacrifices we may offer through lifestyle worship are not unnoticed by God. He sees them all, and He will not let them go unrewarded. In fact, our giving garners greater gain!

Be patient, though. Temporal life is a blink compared to eternity, when our true gains are realized. Consider Moses:

"By faith Moses, when he had grown up, refused to be known as the son of Pharaoh's daughter. He chose to be mistreated along with the people of God rather than to enjoy the pleasures of sin [e.g., the luxury and prestige in Egypt's royal palace] for a short time. He regarded disgrace for the sake of Christ as of greater value than the treasures of Egypt, because he was looking ahead to his reward" (Heb. 11:24-26).

Features of Lifestyle Worship

An important part of our transformation into lifestyle worshipers then is the renewal of our minds regarding the world and our worship. We gain God's perspective by digging into God's Word. Therein we find five features of lifestyle worship:

1. Lifestyle worship is simple, not complicated.
2. Lifestyle worship welcomes heart, not formula.
3. Lifestyle worship is daring, not dull.
4. Lifestyle worship is a process, not an event.
5. Lifestyle worship focuses on giving, not receiving.

What is your personal assessment at this moment? Is your focus on yourself? Do you have a feeling of personal barrenness? If so, then remind yourself *now* that where you are is just a starting point. Your barrenness can break into blossom again.

Here's to fruitful trees, no matter how barren they look right now.

The next chapters explore the transforming renewal of mind that God makes possible when we are properly centered on Him. We'll also look at another person in the hallway of portraits whose confidence in God was put to the ultimate test.

Chapter 10

Taking Aim at Angst

❦

Far too many Americans are being crucified these days. The cross is made of two beams: stress and anxiety. And the two piercing stakes? Yesterday's regrets and tomorrow's worries.

This cross, serviced by these stakes, drains our time, our talent, and our treasure mercilessly. Satan, our accuser, loves it; it helps him forget another Cross which dealt him a crushing and eternal blow.

Our society, in fact, is soaked in anxiety. An estimated twenty-million-plus Americans have some psychophysiological disease in which anxiety is a major player. Angst, in fact, leads the pack: Anxiety is widely regarded as society's number one mental disorder.[5]

For a vivid reminder of this, let's watch some video clips of Suzy, an All-American girl.

Clip #1: Suzy's first nine months are literally a wonder! Look at that young marvel, safely tucked in Mommy's tummy, warm, well-nourished, and well-protected. With not a care in the world and nothing much to do, her greatest adventure is sucking her lilliputian thumb.

Clip #2: Suddenly one day, Suzy gets the surprise of her short life. A spontaneous series of spasms squeezes her tiny body. One after another they come, inch by inch moving her relentlessly closer to an ominously small opening. Like Minnie Mouse tied to a conveyor belt moving toward a tree-mulching machine, Suzy comes nearer and nearer to that teensy weensy slot. The thumb comes out of her delicate mouth. "Woe is me!" she wails silently.

Clip #3: Dismay turns to panic as she is slowly swallowed by that opening. Rudely and repeatedly, she is thrust along. Once beyond the mouth, Suzy finds herself encased in a slippery, skintight tube that literally bends her out of shape. Her beautiful head takes on the shape of a huge peanut. "What did I do to deserve this?" she moans.

Clip #4: Finally and mercifully, light appears at the end of the tunnel. Then Suzy experiences a sudden rush of brand new experiences: bright light, cool air, new noises. Actually, it is a time of brand spanking new experiences: Suzy jumps as the doctor slaps her little seat. Offended and alarmed, she cries out at this affront to her personal dignity—and is startled by another new sound: herself!

Just when she is starting to relax and almost enjoy the coddling of the noisy behemoths dressed in white, one of them suddenly squirts a stinging solution into Suzy's eyes.

Ouch! More pain and alarm. "Just a precaution," the nurse says blandly.

What, pray tell, can you expect from life when it begins with so much angst in so short a slice of time?

Clip #5: Early years have flown by, and Suzy now approaches school age. "We don't want our little Suzy to be deprived," her parents say resolutely. Determined to avert that disaster, Mom coaches Suzy in reading, teaches her to write, and sends her to pre-kindergarten school to learn pre-algebra and impressionistic art.

Ballet lessons, piano lessons, and soccer games round out the schedule for Suzy. Her turbo-charged supermom is also employed thirty hours per week at a local boutique, has two other children (with their schedules), is a discussion leader at the local Henry David Thoreau club ("for my own relaxation") and sings in the church choir.

Oh! Here are more clips of Suzy, showing her as she grows up through adolescence. Do you see her catching more anxieties common to the culture: her self-conscious comparisons with other girls' faces, figures, and fashions; her competition for the acceptance, friendship, and affection of significant others; the dilemma of separating wheat from chaff among boys; the uncertainty about which high school curriculum to choose for which kind of college to attend—then where to go and what to major in and whom to marry (if anybody) and what God's will is for Suzy's life and. . . .

More years pass. Our last video catches another mom and child running from one activity to another in high gear. Mom's eyes are determined, her brow furrowed, and her palms clammy.

At first glance, it looks like a rerun of clip #5. And so it is—almost: This time, the supermom is Suzy. And the beat goes on. . . .

You and I understand Suzy, because we've been through some of these things ourselves. Dads and sons get as captured as mothers and daughters in this pathetic tragicomedy. The "hurried child" is but one of many societal symptoms of stress and anxiety.

Unless we handle these and other concerns properly, we can be drawn under, engulfed as wave after wave of anxiety crashes down upon us like pounding surf. The effects can be devastating.

Unwrapping Anxiety

The good news is that we only put up with this situation for seventy or eighty years. Can you imagine living in today's world for 969 years, as Methuselah lived in his?

Anxiety is defined in psychological literature as a transitory condition characterized by a subjective, consciously perceived sense of tension, apprehension, and elevated autonomic nervous system activity of varying intensity.

Webster's Dictionary defines it as "uneasiness and distress about future uncertainties," appropriately connecting the condition to concern about things to come. We sometimes call it "worry."

Anxiety is associated with—but distinct from—depression. The main difference is their orientation: anxiety, as explained above, is concerned about the future, whereas depression is tied to the past.

Anxiety is linked very closely with fear. However, fear itself usually has an object: You are traveling at the speed limit on a freeway and suddenly see brake lights and swerving cars immediately ahead. You hit your brakes and look frantically for a safe lane change because you are appropriately afraid of crashing into the cars ahead of you. You fear a specific, unpleasant, traumatic outcome.

In contrast, anxiety is feeling the emotion of fear, but not knowing what it is that you fear. That uncertainty, that ambiguity, is considered a key distinction.

That's why it is often so helpful, when we sense anxiety about some particular matter, to ask ourselves, "What is the worst that can happen if I take or do not take this action?"

If we identify the worst-case scenario and decide that we can probably handle it, exposing anxiety to the truth causes it to melt and then evaporate. That releases more energy and more focused attention to devote to productive use.

Be encouraged by the fact that a certain dosage of anxiety is okay. It can motivate you to study well for a test, to prepare for a speaking engagement, and to practice for an athletic or musical event. In these and similar situations, anxiety is telling you that you have a challenge to conquer; it stimulates you to take action.

Other times, anxiety is helpfully alerting you to something inside which needs to be confronted. Are you angry about something or at someone? Did someone offend you? Do you feel guilty about something? These unresolved issues also trigger anxiety until they get the attention they need.

Assessing the Damage

However, when sustained too long or at too high a level, anxiety becomes cancerously negative. Our minds are affected. Anxiety clouds our understanding, destabilizes our attitudes and scrambles our values.

Our emotions are affected. Joe thrashes others with his words; Jay lashes out with his fists; Jane sulks.

Our bodies are affected. It hurts our hearts, intensifies our tiredness, and reduces our resistance to various diseases.

In fact, systematic research has revealed sobering information about the effects of stress. Here are some of the possible consequences on a person who experiences excessive stress over a prolonged period of time: panic or anxiety attacks, higher cholesterol, increased blood pressure, heart attacks, physical exhaustion, insomnia, strange body sensations ("parathesias"), unexplainable pain, skipped heartbeats, irritability, accidents, alcoholism, drug addiction, strained relationships, apathy, poor judgment, reversals in usual behavior, headaches, indecisiveness, withdrawal, loss of perspective, paranoia—and this list is not exhaustive, even if exhausting.

Our jobs are affected also. Long hours, stress to perform maximally, and the constant jockeying for position combine to produce long-term dullness, mediocrity, and/or disability. Sounds like burnout time. . . .

Then the law of diminishing returns comes out to play with the Peter Principle. And what happens? Your company sends you out to pasture, brings in a fresh living sacrifice, and starts the cycle again.

Our marriages are affected too. With all due respect to the "one flesh" mystique, marriage is a covenanted but uncompleted meltage of two very distinct individuals. Each brings his or her own "baggage" (quirks, expectations, reactions, phobias, anxieties, effects of positive/negative experiences and associations, etc.) to this relationship. That in itself creates quite a dynamic environment!

As they then interact with each other—and with each other's baggage—the anxiety potential climbs exponentially as they "bear one another's burdens." These anxieties generate more anxiety. Anxiety compounds, feeding on itself.

This buildup grows much like compound interest earnings. However, the results are taxed at a much higher rate: Uncontrolled anxiety can be the death of a marriage.

Our children are also affected. We are their role models, like it or not. We can be good models or we can be bad, but we cannot be non-models. They watch us daily and absorb us daily. What goes in will eventually come out in their lives, in one form or another.

A dramatic example comes from Sheila Ribordy, a clinical psychologist and professor at DePaul University. An eight-year-old boy was referred to her because he would become easily and extremely anxious if his class work did not match his expectations.

She discovered why. This third grader should have been spending thirty to forty-five minutes a day on his homework. Instead, he was putting in three hours per day. Why? Because he was afraid he would disappoint his parents. He reread and rewrote his assignments over and over.

His parents were shocked, since they had never told him to put himself under such pressure. That made no difference to the boy. This young, uptight overachiever—not unlike Suzy—simply saw his parents as his models. Dad was a business executive, a successful perfectionist. Mom was highly educated, but she had left her career to literally pour herself into her children. Their son not only followed their example, but he feared that they would emotionally disown him if he failed to excel at everything. And they had never said a mumbling word. . . .

We are also our children's security blanket. If they see us and our marriages unraveled by anxiety, it shakes their own sense of security right down to the core of their young beings. ("Bad things only happen to bad people. This is a bad thing. If this is happening to me, I must be a bad boy. . . .") Who can predict the profound consequences of that quake?

What can we learn from this? Sustained anxiety may make more dollars for a moment, but it makes no sense.

What can we do about this? Quite a bit, as you will discover in the next chapter.

Chapter 11

Turning Worry into Worship

❦

Do we all have the same capacity to become "worry warts"? Are all people equally apt to be anxious?[6]

No, some are more angst-prone than others. One key factor is a person's sense of security. One of Satan's prime ploys for luring us into the trap of negative anxiety is insecurity. The less secure we are, the more likely we are to become unhealthily anxious.

Unsure of ourselves, we try to bolster our ego with I'm-the-best or I'm-worth-it declarations. Unsure of how others see us, we make look-how-well-I'm-doing and see-how-important-I-am statements.

These statements are seldom verbalized outright. More often, we communicate them indirectly by accumulating status symbols for people to notice or by dropping important names into our conversations.

All this is done in the desperate and pathetic hope that others will be impressed with who we know, what we do, or what we've accomplished. It's a sad admission that we think our personal value hinges on our association with important people or important events. God views our value so differently!

The hidden motive driving many of us to the top of our various endeavors is insecurity. It is the craving to be noticed and accepted, the yearning for a respect that we perhaps do not have for ourselves.

Research supports this analysis. Psychiatrist Roy Grinker, for example, conducted some "normality studies" in Chicago which showed a significant link between anxiety and achievement.[7]

Minirth, Meier, and Hawkins authored a very helpful book, *Worry-Free Living*,[8] which addresses anxiety from biblical, medical and psychological perspectives. They point to another variable which helps identify those most likely to succeed (that is, be angst-prone): personality.

Those with "Type A" personalities, known by psychiatrists as obsessive-compulsives, are prime candidates for stressful anxiety. Generally, Type A's can be described as intelligent, perfectionistic, seldom overlooking details, a bit obstinate.

They are usually dedicated workers, neat in appearance, and orderly in work habits. They tend to be logical, more facts-oriented than feelings-oriented, good problem-solvers and competitive. They are a little adversarial too, likely to take an opposing view, and build a good case just for the fun of it.

Type A's set high goals, work like dogs to reach them, feel crushed if unable to, have no tolerance for mediocrity, and have the same unrealistic expectations of others that they do of themselves. Of course, unrealistic expectations lead to frustration—which leads to even more anxiety!

As if these tendencies were insufficient in themselves to create high anxiety in the Type A, the Type A operates like this in an environment that itself is stressful. He or she often selects a career characterized by challenge, extensive training, and stress. Medicine, the pastorate, and certain business tracks are good examples.

Consumed by work, driven to achieve, guilty about relaxing—you know the type and readily see their predisposition to anxiety. Fortunately, there are ways to escape the anxiety trap—even for Type A's.

Another variable may surprise you: birth order. As Minirth et al. point out, firstborns are most likely to have Type A personalities. They tend to be conscientious, achievers, jealous of attention given to younger siblings, angrier than their siblings, tense, and driven by the high expectations of parents, who relax more as other children come along.

Firstborns tend to make friends more slowly than their siblings, and as loners, consequently, they are less comfortable sharing their feelings with friendly sounding boards. Schoolmates are seen as rivals, not confidants. Their harbored emotions and worries do them no favors.

Dealing with Anxiety

Whether we are Type A's or not, how—as part of renewing our minds—can we deal successfully with anxiety? How can we turn worry into worship?

One step we need to take early in the process is to detect defense mechanisms we are using to fool ourselves or others. "I'm just going to do it this once. . . ." "This isn't hurting me/us." "Everything is fine. . . ." "Honey, this is only temporary; pretty soon I'll be able to slow down."

Well has God said through the prophet Jeremiah, "The heart is deceitful above all things and beyond cure. Who can understand it?" (17:9).

"Search me, O God, and know my heart," David prayed, "test me and know my anxious thoughts. See if there is any offensive way in me, and lead me in the way everlasting" (Ps. 139:23-24).

The book of Proverbs admonishes, "Above all else, guard your heart, for it is the wellspring of life" (4:23). When our guard is down, deception can creep in. We need God's searchlight, shining the truth into our hearts and chasing away self-delusions. Guarding our hearts and detecting self-deceit are two disciplines in the worship of abiding.

How does God help us detect deceit? Just as He helped me through my winter experience, first He takes us to His Word: "For the word of God is living and active. Sharper than any double-edged sword, it penetrates even to dividing soul and spirit, joints and marrow; it judges the thoughts and attitudes of the heart" (Heb. 4:12).

Second, He brings friends to our side. Loving, frank friends are an invaluable blessing. "But encourage one another daily, as long as it is called Today, so that none of you may be hardened by sin's deceitfulness" (Heb. 3:13).

Third, as we engage in the worship of abiding, He nourishes us and sensitizes us to defense mechanisms which are quenching His work in our lives.

Strategically, we *do* want the kind of anxiety that somehow helps us. A little anxiety can help motivate us to study for a test or perform at our best in sports. What we *don't* want is the kind that hurts us. This is our concern at the moment.

In certain situations, however, negative anxiety has a positive end product. For example, God may create anxiety within you to get your attention about an unresolved problem. If you face that problem, deal with it, and then get on with living, the anxiety has helped you conquer that problem!

If you and I respond that way, we will "cap" the anxiety, preventing it from getting to the level at which it hurts us. That is part of the process of abiding.

Strategy for High Anxiety

How can we put that strategy into a more workable approach? These steps are generalized to keep them simple. However, don't treat them lightly. They can add health to your bones and restore joy to your life.

To relieve high anxiety, we take these steps:

1. Identify the hidden emotion causing the angst.
2. Air out the problem; talk it out with a trustworthy confidant; understand it enough to deal with it.
3. Resolve the problem and reconcile with other partici-pants in the problem, even if they do not respond in kind; apologize or do whatever necessary.
4. Forgive every offense committed by others involved. Refuse to let your mind dwell on the offense or on personal revenge. Release it and let God renew your mind.

To prevent high anxiety, consider these as practical suggestions for the worship of abiding:

- Read and reflect on Scripture—particularly noting what it reveals about God. Sometimes our anxiety is simply—and profoundly—a lack of abiding, a lack of intimacy with God.
- View your problems through worship lenses. God's perspec-tive can take the angst out of day-to-day tensions.
- Replace panic with prayer.
- Obey Him. It's amazing how much anxiety can be prevented simply by doing what is right and avoiding what is wrong!

- Sometimes our anxiety is rooted in a sense of worthlessness. Recognize and rehearse the truth about yourself (Rom. 12:3): You are deeply loved by God as you are! Why would Christ have sacrificed His life for you, if you were not worth it? Reject those negative thoughts about yourself and replace them with that wonderful truth.

- Talk through problems with a trusted group before anxiety reaches crisis levels. Consider how these verses apply here: "And let us consider how we may spur one another on toward love and good deeds. Let us not give up meeting together . . . but let us encourage one another . . . " (Heb. 10:24-25).

- Get sound, professional help if necessary. Sometimes anxiety is simply a medical problem.

- Listen to soothing music. Human response to music is convincingly documented; we are affected psychologically and physiologically. Even King Saul, wart that he became, knew and used the music therapy that came from David's harp!

- Take a break. Come aside, as Jesus did with his disciples. Get away from people and rest a while.

- Plan only 60 percent of your day. Interruptions will take care of the rest, and you will be less frustrated.

- Take a daily time out. Spend twenty minutes, apart from Bible study, etc., thinking Philippians 4:8 thoughts. Think about things in your world that are noble, are honorable, are lovely, are pure, are true, are excellent, are praiseworthy. God will bless such thinking with the promise of verse 9: peace.

- Exercise regularly. The benefits are legion.

It's Your Life

Remember insecurity, one of the driving variables in both success and anxiety? Let me close with a brief, true story.

In the early years of the twentieth century, a large immigrant family left their homeland and sailed across the ocean from Europe to America. When they finally arrived in the new country, they worked their way through many major adjustments. They had to learn English, they had to find employment, they had to have housing, and they had another baby.

Nicknamed "Buster," this child certainly threatened to do just as his nickname suggests to the family finances.

Buster's early years could have given him good reason to feel insecure. While he was still a child, his father was killed in a construction accident. His mother died at about the same time, the victim of a serious illness.

By the age of nine, Buster was an orphan. Tossed from one older sibling to another—none of whom had any great desire to take him in—he grew up with no real home nor real acceptance.

His older brothers and sisters did not particularly hide their reluctance to house him. One Christmas, while living with an older sister, Buster and his sister's son, Charles, each found a Christmas stocking hung for them over the fireplace. Both were filled with treats for the boys. Christmas day arrived, and they excitedly took down their stockings and looked inside.

For Charles, there were candies, sweet bread, and other goodies for him to enjoy. For Buster, chunks of charcoal. "We don't want you!" the charcoal shouted.

What kind of adult emerges from that kind of childhood? When I became acquainted with Buster, by now called "Bud," he was a successful businessman, a devoted husband, and a loving father. Graciously, he had fully forgiven his family. They, in response, now warmly welcomed him into their homes. Holidays often found him and his young family happily visiting his brother and sisters. To his only son, he gave the middle name "Charles."

He was a gifted singer. One of his favorite songs explains the cause of this counter-cultural behavior. The song, drawn from Ephesians chapter 1, took on new meaning for me as, little by little, he reluctantly recounted his past:

> In the Beloved, accepted am I;
>> Risen, ascended and seated on high;
>> Saved from all sin through His infinite grace;
>> With the redeemed ones, accorded a place.
>> In the Beloved, God's marvelous grace
>> Calls me to dwell in this wonderful place.

God sees my Savior, and then He sees me,
In the Beloved, accepted and free.[9]

Bud, who had good reason to feel very insecure, was instead very assured, nourished in the knowledge that he was fully accepted by Christ, his Beloved. Accepted and free, he was free to live, free to forgive, and free to serve his Beloved.

He did just that, first as a Sunday school teacher, then on various ministry teams, next as a foreign missionary, and later as a pastor in California. Bud's body wore out over the years; it couldn't keep up with his spirit. I was privileged to speak at his funeral, which was really our celebration of his freedom from bondage to a burdensome body.

I told the group that gathered that day about his stress-laden childhood. I told about his premature deprivation of parental love and care and about his life as an orphan. I told about the chunks of charcoal and the message they conveyed. Then I played a tape of him singing that song.

If you were to visit that humble grave in Escondido, California, you would see a small stone marker. Carved on that marker is the four-word message trumpeted in my father's life: "Accepted in the Beloved."

So, my Christian friend, are you.

Chapter 12

Keeping Up with the Joneses

❦

Today we not only carry the anxieties common to mankind since Adam and Eve, but we live in a world system that *encourages* anxiety as a way of life.

At work, competitive anxiety within the company is consciously programmed into the corporate culture. Some senior executives intentionally throw selected junior executives together. Why? Like a cockfight, they want to stir up professional rivalry in the hope that the company will somehow advance as these junior execs anxiously jockey for position and perks.

In sales, figures for last year, last quarter, last month, and even last week are posted at headquarters and distributed to all the reps, so everyone can see who this moment's golden kid is—and who the goats are, that is, everyone else. Why? A little anxiety leverage may boost sales for the company.

In law, two attorneys, neither wanting to be outmaneuvered by the other, scheme tenaciously to convince the court of their view, regardless of the right or wrong done by the defendant.

Managers are much more likely to applaud than reprimand their employees for long hours on the job. In addition to public praise, financial and perk incentives are given for higher and higher production, giving a green light to the go-for-it types who are most vulnerable to these ploys.

Almost inevitably, these chargers experience increased anxiety at work and increased anxiety at home. Their motivation is clear: "I'm not gonna let Harry look better than me." or "Honey, I'll have to work again this Saturday, but it's only temporary. It'll be worth it when I get promoted."

Is this only a marketplace mentality? No. Remember Suzy's superparents? The fear of causing Suzy to forgo future opportunities drove them and Suzy into an incessant flurry of must-do activities.

The advertising industry has capitalized on our weakness, propelling us cleverly from the keep-up-with-the-Joneses mentality to a new high: keep-ahead-of-the-Joneses.

At home, our kids want their friends' best toys, nicest clothes, and favorite compact discs. Mom and Dad don't want to appear neglectful, so they comply. After all, kids are only kids once, right?

Wrong. We adults are just older kids. As someone has aptly observed, the difference between men and boys is the cost of all their toys. *We do no better although we do know better.* We want a nest egg like our parents', but we also want a house like Harry's and Hazel's, a car like Bob's and Betty's, a wardrobe like Sam's and Sally's, and a marriage like Tom's and Tammy's.

The undercurrent in this phenomenon is often not the joy of moving forward so much as the fear of plateauing or falling behind. As stated earlier, often anxiety pushes us to climb higher, regardless of how that climb is scored. Whoever said that peer pressure was only an adolescent dynamic?

What Is a Person Like You Doing in This Place?

Why? How do we get into these complicated, confusing, conflicting, expensive situations? The gate is wide, and many there be who enter. Above the gate are two words: imprudent comparisons.

Eve looked at the fruit of the tree in the middle of the garden, compared it with other fruit in her experience, decided she wanted it, and bought it without remotely knowing the price she would have to pay. Adam looked at Eve, compared the pluses of going along with her to the minuses of disagreeing with her, and replied, "Whatever you say, dear." And so has it ever been.

Comparisons, of course, are not inherently bad. In the marketplace we are wise to compare products and select the option best suited to our needs and circumstances. In relationships we are *very* wise to choose friends—especially marriage partners—with care. Such decisions require discerning comparisons.

The problem, again, is imprudent comparisons. These come in at least two different models. One model is the incomplete comparison. Hazel's house is beautiful, but what income is required to support it? Bob's car is the envy of all car lovers, but what has he shortchanged to free up funds for it?

Jim's success in corporate climbing is outstanding, but does he know his children? Don is scaling the heights in sales, with its accompanying company kudos and coveted compensation. Do his accomplishments have any connection to his three marriages? Our comparisons often ignore the whole picture of those with whom we compare ourselves.

The second model is the incongruent comparison. If I compare myself to Bruce and berate myself for not matching or better yet exceeding his accomplishments, it is time for me to take off my sandals: I am stepping off my turf and onto God's holy ground. Are *any* two people identical in spiritual gifts, natural gifts, experiences, resources, and opportunities? Should they be? Must God "bless" both identically?

The answer to these questions is a resounding *no*. And if that is true, then I complicate my life unnecessarily when I insist on imposing on myself an incongruent comparison which shouldn't be and—if it were to be—is God's responsibility rather than mine.

Most of our anxieties are self-imposed, aren't they? What a self-defeating pastime.

Enough said about making the wrong kinds of comparisons. There is another aspect of our thinking which also needs renewal. For reasons you will quickly understand, let's call this our tendency to *dote* on the wrong dimension.

Externalities and Internalities

Gail Sheehy, in *Passages: Predictable Crises in Adult Life*, describes life in terms of its external and internal dimensions.

Your external dimension includes such "cultural memberships" as your job, your social class, your role within that social class, your family, and your role within that family. Your external dimension also includes the way you present yourself to those around you and the way you participate with those around you. It is your outer self.

Your internal dimension includes the meanings this interaction has for you: your feelings, your values, your goals, your aspirations. It is your inner self.

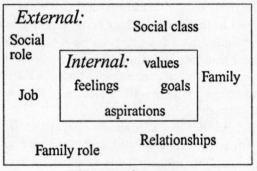

Competing dimensions

These two dimensions compete within each of us for our attention—and which wins, do you think? Right. The external.

Why? Probably because the steps of our inner growth are more difficult than those for our outer growth. "What's more," Sheehy says so well, "the prizes of our society are reserved for outer, not inner, achievements. Scant are the trophies given for reconciling all the forces that compete to direct our development, although working toward such a reconciliation . . . is what underlies all growth of the personality."[10]

Another way to describe this is in terms of the battle between doing and being. We generally opt for the easier: We *D*well *O*n *T*he *E*xternals (*dote*). It is this mental *dote*ing that generates the unwise comparisons detailed above.

One example of such a person is Zacchaeus, a short man whose short story occurs in Luke 19. As Jericho's chief tax collector, he may not have been well liked, but he certainly had power. Ambitious, he had even climbed to the position of chief collector. To his achievements he added the accumulation of wealth. Externals mattered a great deal to him. He was a *doter*.

Then he met Jesus. That encounter revolutionized his perspective, changed his heart, and led him to give half of his possessions to the poor and to handsomely repay anyone he had cheated. On what, do you suppose, was he dwelling thereafter?

Advertisers have been very quick to exploit our *doteing* for their corporate profit. Have you seen the TV commercial surrounding a jar of mustard with an environment of luxury? If you are willing to accept the *association* they are trying to create between their mustard and that environment, they are willing to accept your money!

How about the nauseating ads which try to build in our minds an association between cigarettes or beer—dirt to our lungs and death to our lives—and cleanliness, youth, freshness, and fun? Can dwelling on those external trappings affect our thinking and purchasing habits? Count on it; the promoters are.

In contrast, there's the *Reader's Digest*. Issue after issue contains articles which challenge you to *Dwell On The Internals (DOTI)*. That has a good ring to it, your conscience reminds you. Like a recurring ulcer, more internal conflict (anxiety) is triggered by that acknowledgment, as you wrestle with the dilemma between *dote-ing* and *dotiing*.

Dr. Luke gives us an example of the *doti* person too. In chapter 18 of his Gospel he tells of a rich ruler approaching Jesus with a question. He has it all: wealth, position, prestige, youth and more: high moral standards. His question (as yours and mine might be if we had what he had): "How can I live forever?"

Christ's answer is not what he wants to hear. In stark contrast to Zacchaeus, the young man sadly walks away from Jesus. Having attained his goals in the external and internal arenas, his vision has stopped at that internal step and he climbs no higher even when Christ offers him the opportunity.

Conflicting Interests

And you? Then comes Sunday. You go to church and hear a sermon telling you to dwell neither on externals nor on internals but on *eternals*.

What? Another dimension? This is too confusing . . . nothing fits together . . . gimme the old-time externals. At least I can see and grab hold of them. . . .

This conflict of values results in a conflict of goals. Goal conflicts produce weakness of resolve. Weak resolve triggers conflicting actions. Suddenly you see yourself as a ship with a very confused captain and compass, going one direction and then another, maybe enjoying the cruise—but certainly getting nowhere. Your life is one of frustrated insignificance.

The springtime of your life passes, then the summertime. Then you enter the winter of your life and look back in dismay, "Where did the years go? What have I done that really matters? Why did I do this to myself?"

Consider Solomon's poignant words: "And I saw that all labor and all achievement spring from man's envy of his neighbor. This too is meaningless, a chasing after the wind" (Eccl. 4:4).

That, of course, is just where Satan wants us. He has declared spiritual warfare against us. He wants us either neutralized or destroyed. To that end he works diligently as our tempter, deceiver, and accuser.

No wonder we are called sheep. Sheep certainly have their commendable points, but intelligence does not appear to be one of them.

I remember hearing a story of some men who were unloading sheep from a boat. As the sheep came down the ramp, the workers held a staff across the ramp. The first sheep dutifully jumped the staff and continued onward. The second did the same and so did the third.

Then the men withdrew the staff. Wouldn't you know it, the rest of the sheep kept jumping the nonexistent barrier as if the staff were still there! Mindless conformity.

The Way Through the Wilderness

Do you want to be a mindless conformist like that? I doubt it, or you wouldn't be reading this book.

God has the answer. My Lord knows the way through the wilderness. Again we come back to Romans 12: "Do not conform any longer to the pattern of this world, but be transformed by the renewing of your mind. Then you will be able to test and approve what God's will is—his good, pleasing and perfect will" (v. 2).

Paul underscores this thought in another letter: "Since, then, you have been raised with Christ, set your hearts on things above, where Christ is seated at the right hand of God. Set your minds on things above, not on earthly things" (Col. 3:1-2).

With His Holy Spirit helping us, we need to renew our minds daily and repeatedly. As we so discipline ourselves, our thoughts and wills will be transformed, purged more and more of their tendency to dwell on externals and purposed more and more to dwell on eternals.

What is the result? Our renewed values will not conflict with each other. Our goals will be in alignment. Our resolve will be—and must remain—strong, for Satan will not take this sitting down. Our behavior will be—and must remain—consistent and energized.

"And when we fail?" you ask. God has provided for that: We repent; He forgives. We may have to deal with the consequences, but we do so knowing that He no longer holds our failure against us. That simplification significantly and profoundly helps us shift our attention from our culpability to our cope-ability.

Disentangled from conflicting and distracting goals, our energy can now be focused with greater intensity on the actions God directs us to take. That simplification significantly and profoundly enhances our capability.

Equipped with this mind-set and heartset, our lives, like ships, will sail in significant paths whether the weather be stormy or calm. Why? Because we—through continuous renewal—are directed by only one Captain and only one compass, His Word.

Does this strategy seem beyond reach? Are we talking "pie in the sky"? "No," say men and women throughout the Bible. Another walk down the hallway of portraits will give you rest for your soul and encouragement for your pilgrimage.

Creative conformity to Christ is seen by the world around us as nonconformity to its norms. An outstanding Old Testament leader, recommended to us in our interview with the apostle Paul, dramatically lived his faith in God. Let's look in on him next.

Chapter 13

Becoming a Nonconformist

❦

Jehoshaphat was an important man with a big problem. As King of Judah from 872 to 848 B.C., he had position, riches, and honor. It was apparent to those around him that in spite of occasional lapses in good judgment, he definitely enjoyed God's stamp of approval. Surrounding nations took note and left him alone, being filled with "the dread of the LORD" (2 Chron. 17:10).

In addition to his military and governmental leadership, Jehoshaphat played a proactive role in the spiritual leadership of his people. He initiated a series of seminars presented by hand-picked teachers who traveled throughout Judah instructing people concerning the law of the Lord.

He also instituted significant judicial reform, and as he appointed judges, he charged them to let the fear of the Lord be their guide. Don't you wish he could become President of the United States?

A Test of Faith

But one particular day quickly threatened to challenge his skill as a leader. Happily and productively involved in worthwhile causes, Jehoshaphat was suddenly interrupted by a chilling intelligence report: A vast, vicious, foreign army was on its way down to make Judah its pawn.

His predicament was not unlike the 1990 invasion of tiny Kuwait by towering, greedy Iraq. How might you respond in such a situation? Would you race into exile? Hide your assets? Would you run to your allies for rescue? Maybe update your will? Would you ask, "Is this what I get, Lord, for serving you?"

After getting my stomach down out of my throat, my response might be to get eleventy-seven different plates spinning at once in an effort to mobilize my troops, allies, and country for conflict. My tendency would probably be to pray a little and rush a lot from one spinning dish to another.

Jehoshaphat's response was a marvel of faith. Sending word quickly throughout Judah by messengers, he called on the people to fast. That they did, and then they came to Jerusalem to seek help from the Lord. Reflecting their respect for Jehoshaphat and for Jehovah, people came from every town in the kingdom, gathering in front of the new temple courtyard.

Their rendezvous point was significant because this sanctuary had been built with the understanding that if ever they were faced with calamity, they would stand there in God's presence, cry out to the Lord, and He would rescue them. This day was certainly a day of imminent calamity. There, expressing their faith before the Lord, Jehoshaphat and the people stood and prayed.

Note, please, that while they fasted and traveled and stood and prayed, the enemy descended on them rapidly. The nation of Judah was not weapon-making, not alliance-building, not wall-reinforcing, not army-training. Their hopes were pinned to a fast and a prayer. Marvelous!

The king then stood up in the assembly and prayed. He reminded God that His relationship with Judah went back over many generations. He reaffirmed God's sovereignty, His power and His might. He reviewed God's action on their behalf and His promise that this land would continue to belong to them.

Zeroing in on the impending doom that brought them together, he began his Jehoshaphat-to-Jehovah SOS: "As You requested, we spared these enemies when we came from Egypt. Now they've turned on us and want to drive us away from the land You gave us." We understand what he meant: "Lord, is this what we get for obeying You? Is this Your idea of a living sacrifice?" (2 Chron. 20:10-12, author's paraphrase).

His prayer ended with a noteworthy expression of trust: "We do not know what to do, but our eyes are upon you" (2 Chron. 20:12).

God responded to this declaration of dependence with words that were literally to become music to Jehoshaphat's ears: "Do not be afraid or discouraged. . . . For the battle is not yours, but [Mine]. . . . Take up your positions; stand firm and see the deliverance." (2 Chron. 20:15-17).

Awed, Jehoshaphat and his people bowed down and worshiped. Jehovah was still in control, and He cared about them!

Early the next morning, they set out in the direction God sent them. Jehoshaphat's challenge and encouragement to his people that day still rings through centuries of time: "Have faith in God, and you will be upheld. . . . You will be successful."

He underscored his faith by positioning at the head of the army a group of men "to sing to the LORD and to praise Him for the splendor of His holiness" (2 Chron. 20:21). As the men sang, God caused the enemy to destroy itself. By the time Judah's troops arrived, the enemy was completely annihilated. All Judah had to do was pick up the plunder, which was so plentiful that it took three days to collect.

Victory through musicians instead of munitions! Not a life left on one side and not a life lost on the other. Not even the amazing Operation Desert Storm was that successful. Who but Jehovah could orchestrate such a score?

And the people remembered that fact. After collecting wagon-loads of winnings from the predatory wannabes, they paused to praise the Lord. Again, when they arrived back in Jerusalem, they went to the temple for a concert of worship. Because of their faith, Jehovah had upheld them; God had given them success.

Stand Fast

A critically important thread connects this event to you and me. Can you detect a common theme in Jehoshaphat's initial strategy, Jehovah's continuing strategy, Christ's vine-branch parallel (John 15), and Paul's armor analogy (Eph. 6:13-14)?

Here it is: Jehoshaphat challenged the people to *stand fast* before God at the temple. Jehovah then instructed them to *stand fast* before the enemy in the battle. Christ later told His disciples to *remain fastened* to the true Vine. Paul told the church to *stand fast*, protected by the armor of God. The constancy of the command should capture our attention!

What we have here is a countercultural effect of *the worship of abiding*. Standing fast in such situations is an action that defies the world's usual pattern of priorities and practices. It is power-based nonconformity.

What courageous obedience the people showed! What fruitful faith! They made a conscious, willful choice to look to Him for their salvation, instead of seeking surrogates.

Why is this account in our Bibles? God permanently recorded their experience for our encouragement to trust and obey: "For everything that was written in the past was written to teach us, so that through endurance and the encouragement of the Scriptures we might have hope" (Rom. 15:4).

God's strategy has not changed: Now, centuries later, He still tells us to abide in Him and thereby become creative nonconformists, standing fast before the enemy, clothed in the strength of our omnipotent God.

None of us may ever experience anything close to the adventures of Jehoshaphat. It doesn't matter; it's just a detail. The fact remains that God does want us to stand fast before our world.

We cannot accomplish this if we conform to the pattern of this world in which we temporarily live. It requires Spirit-led nonconformity and is impossible without true faith in God. He sets us free from the disabling fear of not following the crowd. He empowers us to be creative nonconformists—not for the sake of self-centered eccentricity, but for the glory of God.

Jehoshaphat as Mentor

Some final observations about this outstanding leader are appropriate. We can learn from this godly nonconformist!

When the pressure was on, "Jumpin' Jehoshaphat"—as he has somehow become misknown—didn't jump at all. He stood firmly, first facing his Protector and then facing his predator. He exchanged frenzy for a fast, replaced hurry with heart.

His decision to stop everything and wait before the Lord is not the stuff of sudden impulse. Only a seasoned worshiper would be so daring.

His decision to wait in worship risked his treasure: his life, his family, his wealth. It utilized his talent: leadership that inspired people to obey him in spite of their panic. It cost him time: precious days, unreclaimable. Life's three T's—treasure, talent, time—were wrapped up in this sacrificial act of worship.

Discerning Reality

We live near Palomar mountain in Southern California. Years ago, a powerful observatory was built on Palomar to study the heavens. Planners thought that the site was far enough away from the lights of Los Angeles to eliminate their interference with light from celestial bodies which the astronomers wished to study.

What might have been true in the 1950s is not so in the 1990s. Los Angeles now extends east to Palm Springs, and San Diego reaches north to intersect that metropolis at Corona. Artificial light has become a substantial interference with study at the Palomar Observatory, mixing with celestial light and obscuring the reality of outer space.

Do you remember Jehoshaphat's final statement in his prayer as he and his people first stood before God in Jerusalem? "We do not know what to do, but our eyes are upon you."

Helen Lemmel recaptured that same theme in a chorus penned decades ago:

Turn your eyes upon Jesus;
Look full in His wonderful face
And the things of earth will grow strangely dim
In the light of His glory and grace.[11]

When, in the course of human events, it becomes obvious that the artificial light of nearby attractions is making it difficult for us to see the far-reaching realities of life, we need to emulate King Jehoshaphat. We need to stop our all-consuming activities and rivet ourselves to God. We need to stand fast and perform the worship of abiding.

What will happen? God will change the tide of light. He will reverse the relentless and progressive interference of artificiality and make the things of earth grow strangely dim. He will free us;

we will no longer be boxed in by the world's system. Our renewed minds will see the bigger picture that God sees. And the name of Jesus will be praised in and through us.

❦

How has humanistic theology influenced you? More than you care to admit? Me, too. Let's examine that inward influence next.

Chapter 14
Being All That You Can Be

❦

Be all that you can be, in the...." Do you recall that commercial? Covering the country, it wrapped its recruitment message in a demographically correct gift box. An opportunity for fulfillment, challenge, and adventure! It was all there to be had.

Baby boomers may be more responsive than any particular age group to such a message. Comprised of those born from 1946 through 1964, the United States Census Bureau estimates that this group to which I belong is over 76 million strong.

When families these boomers parent are included, the total tops 130 million. That's over half the population of the United States and the largest generation of families in the history of the country!

A full treatment of boomers is beyond this study of lifestyle worship. However, we need to look at some prominent boomer attitudes as we grapple with our need to integrate worship with life, since so many of us are either included in or influenced by this tremendous group.

Boomers have been bludgeoned by the constant change and continuous crises which have characterized recent decades. Our moms and dads were involved in World War II and then again in Korea. Russian Sputniks beat us into space, Soviet missiles came to Cuba, and Khrushchev predicted that Communists would raise our children.

High voltage tensions exploded into war in Watts; Chicago erupted into riots. A charismatic president was exalted to immortality by his untimely death, later to be exposed for immorality throughout his life. Martin Luther King, Jr. assassinated. So was

Bobby Kennedy. Our own involvement in Vietnam, in a war that will haunt history, confronted us with troubling questions about our virtue.

And all of this is instantly, vividly, and repeatedly brought into our homes via television and other media. It's been quite a life and it isn't over yet.

These and other major events have profoundly undermined our sense of security and trust. Speaking generally, our response has been a traceable tendency to pull away from institutions we used to trust: governmental processes, party loyalty, company directives, denominational affiliation, church influence and even family expectations.

In their stead, we have placed greater emphasis on ourselves: self-determination, self-reliance, autonomy, independence. Another classic leap from frying pan to fire. This movement has been accelerated by several significant factors.

One factor is our education; we are the best-educated generation in the history of our country. With such comes an openness to new ideas which may not be aligned with traditional values and approaches to life.

Another is today's instant access to information. Satellite hookups have given us unprecedented global awareness. Computer databases have given us unmatched national news and knowledge. Information is power, and the more we have, the less we think we need to depend on others.

Another is our standard of living. Born in America, we have the luxury of self-determination in a way not possible if we were born in the deserts of Ethiopia or the jungles of Bolivia. We have opportunities unheard of in many other parts of the world.

Another factor is our entrepreneurial spirit. More companies have recently been formed than at any other time in our history. During the industrial 1950s, for example, about 93,000 businesses were started. In 1984 alone, 640,000 began. New businesses are beginning at about twice the rate of a decade ago.[12] This spirit is a reflection, in part, of a paradigm for personal success which focuses on living in such a way as to develop one's inner potential.

Honest, Abe ...

None could be happier about this than Abraham. Abraham Maslow, that is. Maslow, who died in 1970, is remembered as a leading advocate of humanistic psychology.

He developed a motivational theory which describes a person's progression from basic physiological needs such as food to self-actualization, seen as one's highest need. When that highest level is reached, a person experiences the fulfillment of his or her greatest human potential.[13] Based on his model, humanistic psychotherapy attempts to help people move through these stages.

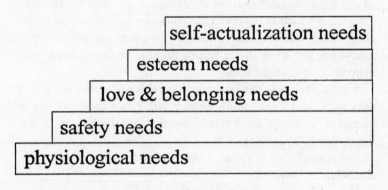

Maslow's motivational theory

The model, as far as it goes, has a compelling logic. Unfortunately for those who have been boxed inside its perspective, it has at least two major flaws.

First, it is two-dimensional. It addresses only the outer self and the inner self; it ignores the eternal self. On second thought, what else would you expect from a humanistic orientation? It is "natural"—perhaps even necessary—for humanists to ignore the reality of eternity, since such confronts them "naturally" with the need to consider God.

Second, it is unattainable. Can we truly be self-actualized on earth? In view of what we have seen of our design in Scripture together, can we even come close to self-actualization when centered on self instead of centered on worshiping God? Was Christ self-actualized on earth?

No, no, and no, according to Philippians 2:3-11.

As a person climbs the Maslow steps, the questions can become a little troublesome: How shall I satisfy my need for love? What do I need to do to feel as if I belong to this group? What should I have or accomplish that will help me raise my self-esteem? Who am I? How can I be all that I can be?

The natural solution is obvious: "Be all that you can be" translates into "Do all that you can do" and "Get all that you can get."

"Meaningless," counters the wise teacher. "A chasing after the wind" (Eccl. 4:4, 8).

He's right, of course. If we let ourselves get into the habit of grasping for such rainbows in our quest for self-actualization and other lesser needs, Satan wins. We compromise our effectiveness—and, not so incidentally, our fulfillment—by allowing such distractions to sidetrack us.

In India, monkey-catchers understand this principle well. When they want to snag a monkey, they put a nut that they know monkeys like into a small box. Then they put the box out where the monkeys will notice it.

Sure enough, an inquisitive monkey comes over to the box, discovers the nut and reaches through the little opening to grasp it. The catcher then comes nearer the box. The monkey sees him, and tries to get away.

No problem, if the monkey lets go of the nut. It can slip its hand out of the opening and escape easily to freedom. But if the monkey continues to grasp the nut, freedom will only be a memory, because the opening in the box isn't big enough for the hand and the nut at once.

Most monkeys, I read, hold on to their prize.

Again, we do no better although we do know better.

When All Else Fails

Maslow made a good start. He recognized and codified much of human need. His error is that he failed to recognize the solution. He looked to the wrong source to supply what we need.

The solution emerges as we survey Scripture, from which selections follow:

- Physiological needs.

   "Do not worry about your life, what you will eat or drink. . . . Look at the birds of the air; . . . your heavenly Father feeds them. Are you not more valuable than they? Who of you by worrying can add a single hour to his life? And why do you worry about clothes? . . . your Heavenly Father knows that you need them. But seek first his kingdom and his righteousness, and all these things will be given to you as well" (Matt. 6:25-33).

- Safety needs.

   "If you make the Most High your dwelling. . . he will command his angels concerning you to guard you in all your ways" (from Ps. 91:9-11).

- Love and belonging needs.

   He tends his flock like a shepherd: he gathers the lambs in his arms and carries them close to his heart; he gently leads those that have young (Isa. 40:11).

   "For I am convinced that neither death nor life, neither angels nor demons, neither the present nor the future, nor any powers, neither height nor depth, nor anything else in all creation will be able to separate us from the love of God that is in Christ Jesus our Lord" (Rom. 8:38).

- Esteem needs.

   For God so loved the world that he gave his one and only Son, that whoever believes in him shall not perish but have eternal life (John 3:16).

- Self-actualization needs.

   Whoever finds his life will lose it, and whoever loses his life for my sake will find it (Matt. 10:39).

   "I consider that our present sufferings are not worth comparing with the glory that will be revealed in us" (Rom. 8:18).

Our internal life develops as we subordinate our external life to our eternal life.

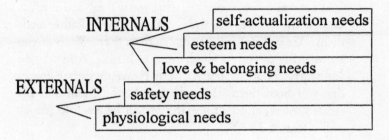

Developing our internal life

This being the case, we come back to Colossians and the issue of *doteing*:

"Since, then, you have been raised with Christ, set your hearts on things above, where Christ is seated at the right hand of God. Set your minds on things above, not on earthly things" (Col. 3:1-2).

The result, in terms of our own lives, is that we, by thinking and functioning as God designed us, will be broader and higher in scope. We'll reach out to those governmental processes, those companies, those denominations and churches, those families.

And by losing ourselves—our coveted autonomy, our self-centered orientation—we find ourselves. Where? Lost in the fulfillment of worshiping Him in very practical ways, worshiping Him as a lifestyle.

❦

The next section focuses on a new aspect of lifestyle worship. We move from an inward look regarding perspective and mind renewal to an outward look at people and needs around us.

How can you and I plug into our worlds effectively? The following chapters focus on that important question.

PART 4: REACHING OUTWARD

Just as each of us has one body
with many members,
and these members do not all have
the same function,
so in Christ we who are many form one body,
and each member belongs
to all the others.
We have different gifts,
according to the grace given us. . . .
(Rom. 12:4-6)

. . . Whatever you do,
do it all for the glory of God.
(1 Cor. 10:31)

Chapter 15

Fulfilling Your Call

❧

How long has it been since someone told you you're special? Whether it was an hour ago or a decade ago, it's true!

The apostle Paul reminded us that we each are God's special work of art: "For we are God's workmanship, created in Christ Jesus to do good works, which God prepared in advance for us to do" (Eph. 2:10).

Think of it: You are a unique work of art—and that not of just any old artist. God Himself crafted you!

He knew you before you were even formed, and had your design in mind before you were even a twinkle in your mother's eyes: "Your eyes saw my unformed body. All the days ordained for me were written in your book before one of them came to be" (Ps. 139:16).

That being the case, it makes sense, as part of our lifestyle of worship, for us to fulfill that design by living in accordance with it. This is our "reasonable service of worship" (Rom. 12:1).

Against this backdrop, reports about job mismatch from professionals who help position and reposition people in the marketplace are profoundly disturbing. Arthur Miller, Jr., is the founder and chairman of People Management, Inc., a firm which for over three decades has worked in this arena. Miller says that job misfit in the work force exceeds 50 percent.

What does that mean? Think of all your friends. Then add all those you only casually know. If Miller's estimate is correct, less than half of the total are plugged into jobs that make substantial use of their strengths and abilities. Could you be one of those?

Miller's statistic may even be conservative. A sixteen-year study of 350,000 employees revealed that only 20 percent were well-placed. The rest—80 percent—had either outgrown their current responsibilities or were stuck in jobs that did not require their talents.[14] What a waste of time, one of life's most precious resources.

Several factors contribute to this tragedy. In varying degrees, one or more of these factors may be operational in all our lives. We would be wise to consider this a "wake up call."

First, it may be the logical consequence of not knowing ourselves very well. Unless we understand how God has gifted us, we should not be surprised that we do not build our careers on those gifts.

Second, we may wander from our design because of the lure of short-sighted philosophies: "Onward and upward"; "He who dies with the most toys wins"; "Your paycheck shows your worth." This emphasis on rank, ownings or earnings is, in fact, rank. It can lead to destructive stress, boredom, and/or profound frustration.

Third, and closely intertwined with these distractions from our design, are expectations. We considered expectations in chapter 8, but in a different context. This time, we will look at those expectations as possible obstacles to our discovery of a fulfilling fit.

If we do not know how God has "wired" us, we are readily susceptible to the frustration of expecting from ourselves something other than that which God designed us to expect. If we choose to ignore our gifts and instead seek some sort of short-sighted success, we again set ourselves up for unfulfillment.

In either case, such eccentric or "off-centered" behavior paves the way to goals which in some areas may be too high or even too low—enter boredom. In others, they may be either broader or narrower than you should reasonably expect of yourself. Sometimes you may set expectations which are quite unrelated to your real design.

Knowing ourselves enables us to filter out some of those distracting and unfulfilling side excursions. Being willing to focus only on work that utilizes and builds our strengths again provides a context in which we can "self-actualize."

Complicating our own knowledge and will are the expectations of "significant others" in our lives. Perhaps your spouse wants you to succeed in a particular endeavor, for whatever reason, that is not in line with your gifts.

Maybe your in-laws are the source of pressure. A friend of mine told me his wife's wealthy parents had never approved of his career—ranching. They wanted their daughter to marry into a more "prestigious" and cultured professional arena.

In truth, both this man and woman love country living, with its livestock, land, and open spaces. He wisely chose to live as he was designed rather than as his in-laws wanted to dictate.

Other times, one's employer is the significant other. The company may stick people into job slots rather than look at personnel as dynamic and expensive resources. They may direct, train, transfer, promote, and evaluate employees without regard to their giftedness.

Then there is the Peter Principle: People will rise to their level of incompetence. That is often what employers do to their personnel. A person good at what he or she does is "elevated" to a higher—and different—position, a position which sometimes does not make use of that person's gifts.

Employees good at building an activity are kept on that project to maintain it. Those good at one project (or plant or product) are "promoted" to multi-project (or multi-location or multi-product) responsibilities. Those good at a local level are promoted to a regional level. Executives who give good advice about turnarounds or other changes are retained to run the organization they served as a consultant.

The results, as people "rise" to their level of incompetence, are lower productivity, higher turnover, lower morale, higher absenteeism, lower enthusiasm, and greater dullness. All these are responses to poor job fit and the consequential stress and distress a poor fit creates.

Who Am I?

So how can we best answer the great question of life: Who am I? There are several variables involved.

For a Christian, there is the question of spiritual gifts. These come to us from God the Holy Spirit. A sampling of them, and nowhere is it inferred that this list is comprehensive, comes from Romans 12, 1 Corinthians 12, Ephesians 4, and 1 Peter 4.

Twenty gifts are mentioned in these passages, most of them given for building up, or edifying, believers. Our understanding of these various gifts comes in part from exegesis and in part from empirical common sense. These gifts, with duplicates eliminated, follow by passage.

Romans 12: Prophecy (preaching, inspired utterance), service (ministry), teaching, encouraging, giving, leadership (authority, ruling, administration), mercy (sympathy, comfort, kindness).

1 Corinthians 12: Wisdom (wise advice and speech), knowledge (studying, speaking with knowledge), faith, healing, miracles, discerning spirits (spiritual discrimination), tongues (speaking in languages never learned, ecstatic utterance), interpretation of tongues, apostleship, helps, administration (governing, getting others to cooperate).

Ephesians 4: Evangelizing, pastoring (shepherding God's people).

One of many reading sources you can use to help identify your spiritual gifts is *Your Spiritual Gifts Can Help Your Church Grow* by C. Peter Wagner.[15]

Another variable in knowing ourselves is our natural gifts. These may include such aptitudes and abilities as sports, art, music, analytical reasoning, dexterity, and conceptual reasoning.

Margaret Broadley's book entitled *Your Natural Gifts* tells us that we each are born with an average of six such aptitudes.[16] Unfortunately, most jobs are said to require only one or two of these, leaving a wide open door for employment dissatisfaction.

Various aptitude tests have been developed to identify these gifts, and can help a person find a properly fitting niche in which to operate. More on that later in this chapter.

Some spend a great deal of time trying to distinguish between spiritual gifts and natural gifts. Don't bother. Who cares? Spiritual or natural, they are gifts—given to you from God. Once you have gained a reasonable understanding of His gifts to you, stop noodling over distinctions and start using them.

A third variable is personality. If you and I had the same set of spiritual gifts and the same set of natural gifts, we may still be quite different individuals because of personality.

Bill, an entrepreneur, seems to need a high level of control over those around him. Jim, a pastor, wants to influence people through persuasion rather than autocratic direction.

Eileen, an executive secretary, works best in an environment characterized by steady routine. Her personality is a contrast to that of Holly, a sales representative who thrives on the flexibility and unpredictability of her schedule.

Paul, an accountant, is careful to dot every *i* and cross every *t* in his work. When coloring with crayons as a child, he probably always stayed between the lines and colored everything on the page before going on to the next picture.

Jack, on the other hand, probably colored a little bit on some pages, skipped others, and in general didn't care a whole lot about lines! Today a real estate developer, he's still a free spirit who would drive procedure-manual writers crazy.

One model used frequently over the years examines personality as revealed through our unique social styles.[17] It looks at how we interact and what we tend to interact with most comfortably. As I describe this, can you see where you are on the grid?

Our pace is estimated along a horizontal continuum, the left side slower and the right side faster. People to the left tend to be the "askers" and people to the right tend to be the "tellers."

Our priority-orientation is estimated along a vertical line. Those in the upper half are more task-oriented and those in the lower half more relationship-oriented, as compared with the population in general.

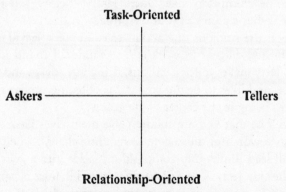

The Social Styles Concept

Task-oriented Askers are characterized as "Analytical" and Relationship-oriented Askers as "Amiable." A typical research scientist would fall into the Analytical quadrant, whereas a person in the Amiable category may be attracted to the field of counseling psychology.

Task-oriented Tellers are considered "Driving," and relationship-oriented Tellers are called "Expressive." A Driving person may enjoy starting her own business, while the Expressive person may find more satisfaction in a sales career.

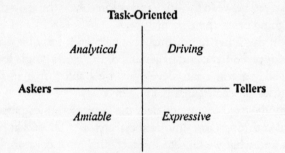

Relationship-Oriented
What is your usual style?

To integrate this perspective with giftedness, imagine for a moment that you have four children. For some of you with bunk beds in your house and a station wagon in the garage, this may be more fact than fantasy!

Each child has a deep interest in and flair for music. Should they all become trumpeters like Uncle Harry? Before you decide, consider other features of your offspring.

Jimmy is the studious one and loves computers. Jackie is Miss Congeniality, diligent in work and a wonderful friend to work beside. Jerry makes quick decisions, is high in energy and low in patience, and likes to be the boss. Jill is outgoing, smiles readily, and likes being in the center of the action.

Could it be that as these children give themselves back to God in lifestyle worship, the self-understanding that you help them gain will lead Jimmy into composition, Jackie into a good choir or orchestra, Jerry into conducting, and Jill into a career or avocation as a vocal or instrumental soloist? Musicians all, yet each quite distinct.

Task-Oriented

Composer - *Analytical* (Jimmy)	Conductor *Driving* (Jerry)
Choral/Orchestral Performer - *Amiable* (Jackie)	Vocal/ Instrumental Soloist - *Expressive* (Jill)

Askers ————————————————— Tellers

Relationship-Oriented

A musical family scenario

Finding Goodness of Fit

I recently visited an elderly friend in the Pacific Northwest. He had asked me to stop by so we could discuss his financial goals and do some appropriate planning.

In the course of our conversation, talk turned momentarily to his career, from which he had retired almost a decade ago. His eyes sparkled and his delightful Dutch accent fairly sang as he described his years as a mechanic on huge Caterpillar tractors.

"Is that why you have all those tool cabinets out in the garage?" I asked. "Yes," he smiled. His pleasure was so obvious that he reminded me of a small child just daring you to ask him what he's holding behind his back.

"What'll it cost me for you to give me a tour of your tools?" I baited him.

"Nothing, as long as you stay with us for dinner," he returned.

For most of the next hour, he showed me the various tools of his trade. Tray after tray was pulled out, everything neatly in its place. His arsenal ranged from huge wrenches that could hardly be lifted except with both hands to tiny dentist's tools which he modified to make it easier to get o-rings out of tight spots.

"You really enjoyed your work, didn't you!" I remarked, observing the obvious. "I most certainly did," he agreed. "Every day, as I began my work, I thanked the Lord for letting me work on these Cats, and I asked Him to make me a blessing to the customers whose Cats I fixed."

"You know," he said wistfully, "I hope there are diesel Cats in heaven. I'd love to spend at least my first fourteen years in heaven working on these things!"

How, as a way of worshiping with your life, can you find a fulfilling fit?

Many tools are available to assist you in the adventure of self-discovery. Some target natural gifts, some spiritual gifts, others interest aptitudes, and so on. Many are interesting and some can be helpful.

You'll notice few mentioned here. Why? Some readers will be like my Dutch friend: No need. He just followed his interests, God opened the doors, and Henry never looked back.

His was the tack taken by men and women throughout the Bible, you may recall! Consider, for example, how well-wired Nehemiah was for his role—not just in rebuilding the Jerusalem walls, but in rebuilding the nation.

A second reason is that some people can get so compulsive about the process that they will be disabled by "analysis paralysis," doomed to spend the next thirty years taking eleventy-seven tests to help them figure themselves out. There's a better-than-even chance that these people are caught in an anxiety trap—or are Analytical Analyticals!

Taking a cue from Miller's System for Identifying Motivated Abilities,[18] let me suggest the following:

- Think back to times of personal joy. What caused each of them?
- Think back to times of satisfying achievement. What did you do, and how did you go about doing it?
- Reflect on compliments you have received. What have others affirmed about you?
- Do more of it.

At this point, you may be thinking more about full-time work in a church or parachurch ministry than about work in the secular arena. While this is laudable, and probably based upon the best of motivations, it may not be the place God wants *you*.

One is not spiritually superior to the other. Clearly from Scripture, God wants His children to be salt and light. That is different from wanting all of us in what is popularly known as "full-time Christian service." Nehemiah was a cupbearer; David was a king. Luke was a physician; Hannah was a homemaker. And the list goes on. . . .

I have a number of friends in "the ministry" whom I'd be very disappointed to see in secular employment. I have other friends, however, who fit into their marketplace so well that for them to leave it for "the ministry" would be a significant loss to both arenas.

You may discover, however, that you are nevertheless engaged in a nonfitting job. Should you quit? Possibly, but don't leap prematurely. You could be jumping from the proverbial frying pan into the fire.

Consider expanding avocationally. You will then have the luxury of exploring options without sacrificing needed finances carelessly.

Is your job dull? Maybe that's just the job you need, because it gives you mental and emotional energy to invest in a church or parachurch ministry that you find is a good fit.

The lifestyle worship of Romans 12 is analogous to the Old Testament "wave offering." (Yes, they did have "The Wave" back in those days!) This offering was waved before the Lord, and presented to Him as a gift. It was then used for God's work and God's workers rather than consumed by fire.

Likewise, our lives are presented to the Lord as an offering. He returns them to us to invest in our "reasonable service of worship."

Who you are is God's gift to you. Who you become is your gift to God. Have you made your life—all that you are, all that you have and all that you will become—a wave offering to Jehovah?

Chapter 16
Burning Out for God

❧

I'd rather burn out for God than rust out!" the pastor boomed from the pulpit. "How about you?"

Larry leaned back in his seat and reflected for a moment. *That's right*, the college senior agreed. *Count me in.*

Larry had worked hard to get through college. Coming from a home where money was adequate for monthly needs but inadequate for post-high-school education, he knew he needed to shoulder both the studying and the funding responsibilities.

And that he did. He worked part-time in a local business, applied for and won a partial scholarship from the university, and also received an educational loan, since he was headed for a teaching career.

After graduating with his teaching credential, Larry began his new life. Still in a classroom, yes, but this time he was presenting the courses and assigning the homework!

Larry sensed a "call" to this field as a professional ministry. He was highly motivated to prove himself and had great expectations of the youngsters he envisioned would be radically transformed by his teaching and personal influence. Pumped up, he literally threw himself into this new challenge.

The junior high school in which Larry taught was staffed with a most supportive group of people. Everyone, it seemed, made him feel welcome and special. The office secretaries were very helpful, the custodial staff was friendly, other teachers shared their secrets for success, and the principal was very encouraging.

Students often stopped to talk with Larry between classes. Some of them were even polite. He was "on his way." A "Teacher of the Year" nomination could not be far off, right?

As time passed, Larry noticed some changes. His teaching colleagues turned their attention more fully to their own work. The following semester, his principal turned down Larry's proposal for a new class he offered to develop and teach.

During his second year, district budget cuts suddenly took away his teacher's aide. That made in-class individualized instruction all but impossible. It also added hours to after-class work such as grading papers and preparing teaching tools.

Then there were the students themselves. Knowing that many came from broken and/or dysfunctional families, Larry had a deep desire to be known as a caring and helpful teacher. He poured himself into the kids, letting them interrupt anything else he might be doing before or after class, before or after school, or during lunch breaks. The students took advantage of his accessibility and after a while there was no escaping them. Larry also took particular interest in several troubled students. He gave of himself tirelessly as a surrogate father/friend/counselor.

Then he discovered that one of them had lied to him about the situation he was trying so hard to help resolve. Another was suspended for drug use, and a third student just didn't care about anything anymore—including Larry.

"If that's how they are going to respond after everything I tried to do to help them," he concluded angrily, "forget it. I don't have time for this."

Gradually his availability to students shrank. Eventually, Larry saw them by appointment only.

Burnout sometimes follows the feeling that we have failed to make our world a better place to live. We haven't really helped the needy. The organization will continue to resist any impact we are trying to make. Our dedication and labor were for naught.

At that point, we no longer seem to have the energy to do what we promised ourselves we would do. We become convinced that we have nothing left to give.

Obstacles to the achievement of our self-expectations may come in the form of inadequate authority. They may involve insufficient resources—finances, time, or personnel. Regardless of the obstacle, frustration can result, paving the road to burnout.

Larry found himself feeling physically de-energized, helpless, disillusioned. He no longer saw himself as the master teacher he had earlier envisioned. For him an almost visible dark cloud hung over the school, over his colleagues, and over life in general.

In spite of this, he pretended that all was well. Of course, this lack of vulnerability backfired. Others around him who could have helped did not know how he really fared. They would have to read his mind to understand his need.

Larry felt isolated. He looked at other educators in similar situations, but they seemed to be doing fine. "I must be the problem," he concluded.

What he missed was *their* masks. They may also have verged on burnout and, looking at him, assumed that he was the one who "had it all together." Oh, the price of the games we play. . . .

Sensing his descent into the quicksand of despondency, Larry fought these feelings, but with less and less conviction. Finally, he simply gave up. "It feels like my soul is dying," he wrote in his personal journal.

With wings of vision clipped and spirit eroded, he ignored the students as individuals. He found it much easier to simply focus instead on lesson plans that covered the course requirements.

He arrived at school each day at the last possible minute and left at the first. Ironically, he gave up caring in order to continue his calling. Four years after entering education as a career, he closed up shop and quit.

So What Is It?

Burnout is formally defined and objectively experienced as a state of physical, emotional and mental exhaustion caused by long-term involvement in emotionally demanding situations. These emotional demands are frequently the result of extreme expectations and sustained situational stresses.

Burnout strikes in a variety of professions: dentists, nurses working with terminal cancer patients, business executives who define themselves by their work, lone pastors of small inner-city churches overwhelmed with needs. Social workers trapped in bureaucratic hassles, endless rules, and meaningless paperwork are also vulnerable.

Its most likely victims are very idealistic and highly motivated individuals who see their work as a calling. When, as with Larry, such a person has given a sustained 133 percent effort to this calling but has not seen the expected results, futility storms the fort.

What a tragedy: The very kind of person we would most want to see in a significant helping profession—someone on fire and eager to make a positive contribution—is most often lost to burnout. Every time it happens to one person, everyone in that sphere of influence is the poorer.

Victimizing expectations can come at three levels. One is general expectations and includes anticipation that our calling will be significant, that we will be allowed to perform our work the way we think best, that we will be an integral member of a group of competent colleagues and that we will be compensated adequately.

A second level is professional expectations and includes achievements which are profession-specific: improving the organization, discovering a cure, solving the problem, bringing opposing forces into agreement, building a better widget, saving more lives, rescuing the world. . . .

The third level is personal expectations. Whether spawned by an admired significant other or by a key experience, these expectations inspire an idealized image of the person we will become in that profession. We envision ourselves in an environment of continued challenge which stimulates our self-actualizing growth.

Does this mean that high expectations are wrong? No.

A poor job fit, discussed earlier in chapter 15, can also lead to burnout. This happens when a person's work does not allow for the expression of his or her giftedness and frustration builds up to that person's burnout point. That is, under-utilization can lead to the same destination as overload.

Another contributor to burnout is oversupervision. (Managers, take note.) One of the blessings of adulthood is control over choices. We want to choose where we'll live and choose where we'll work. We cherish our privilege of driving where we want to go. One of the more difficult rites of passage for an elderly

American is to give up that driver's license or have it taken away against his or her will.

This same dynamic emerges in our work environment. If we have reasonable decision-making authority, we feel better able to cope with the stresses and challenges of work. If too many of those decisions are made instead by our supervisor, we begin to feel that everything we do is governed, observed, and/or evaluated by our supervisor.

Then what happens? You know if you've been there: Morale and motivation plummet faster than the Titanic sank.

It can, of course, get worse. We can lose our jobs. Studs Terkel, in his book entitled *Working*, reported that being fired is one of the most extreme forms of loss of control. Some of us know about that, don't we!

How Shall We Then Respond?

While acknowledging the complex nature of burnout and recognizing that volumes have been written on it, let's look at this problem through worship lenses.

If you sense burnout, it may be caused by yourself or your situation. If you decide that it is yourself, you may feel inadequate, inferior, and incompetent. You may want to quit and re-tool for an entirely different career.

That may not be all bad. Could it be that you *are* in the wrong line of work? Whether because of poor fit or simply a need to fulfill other giftedness, a person is much more likely now than in earlier generations to engage in several careers over a working lifetime. Don't avoid a change that represents a better fit.

In balance, however, don't rush into a different job or career or run away from problems you need to face. Changes can be traumatic and should be made only when well-advised.

Burnout can be one of those crises that triggers significant personal growth. It can force you to reexamine your gifts and your priorities, leading you to a "sober judgment" of yourself (Rom. 12:2-3 again!) that uncovers the foundation upon which you should build your lifestyle of worship.

Maybe you know how God has gifted you, and your situation needs to be modified to fit the work God intends you to do. Maybe your present work environment needs only a small change.

It may mean climbing or not climbing the administrative ladder. Just be sure, if you begin supervising others who enter the kind of work that burned you out, that you provide wisdom for those newcomers rather than cynicism. It's a chance to become a welcomed mentor.

Another way to modify the situation, if your work itself cannot be modified, is to find outside activities that balance your work. Explore new hobbies or help in a church or parachurch ministry that needs your gifts.

Take time for friends. Nourishing friendships are one of God's most wonderful blessings to us. Their support, their love, and their insights are invaluable. The Bible offers many good examples of nourishing friendship; follow these examples—in fact, become one yourself.

As always, a few "don'ts" do help: Don't make the mistake of staying in a burnout mode just because the money is good. That form of seduction you can well afford to avoid. Don't suppose that seeing more patients or getting more clients will solve the problem. You will have even less time for conversations with friends and for outside activities.

Mentioned earlier but worth reiterating: Don't jump to a different organization or a new career without a clear sense of good fit and good timing. That may signal escapism, an issue you need to confront.

Are you a "Type A" personality? This next recommendation may seem strange to others, but Type A's know whereof I speak: Learn to take time to relax and enjoy successful accomplishments. Relish the experience before moving on to meet the next challenge. This, too, can help prevent burnout when you encounter long stretches of desert between accomplishments. The very memory of those times can help sustain your vitality.

If you decide that nothing can be changed in your situation, remember the message of Joseph: Since God is in control, your response is more important than your situation.

When situations cannot be changed, Paul reminds us that we have a formidable weapon against the frustration that breeds burnout: contentment (see Phil. 4:11). Paul had to learn contentment. You can too. Become content with who you are, content with where you are, and content with how you are. Satan doesn't know what to do with contentment!

Another weapon is forgiveness. Guard against bitterness, anger or revenge against any who play a role in your burning out by forgiving them from the bottom of your heart. Forgiveness will deepen you, strengthen you, and will probably add good years to your life.

Our Word for Today Is . . .

The key word in protecting ourselves from burnout is *balance*. We who are sincere Christians and who love God deeply can easily lose our balance.

In fact, our very worship can become unbalanced. How? By hyperserving and hypoabiding.

We can rush out each morning ready to reach the world for Christ, to feed the poor, to visit the widows, to stop the fight, to plan the Sunday school lesson, to build the church, to. . . .

Isaiah rebuked all-consuming service, reminding us that those who wait on the Lord will find their strength renewed (Isa. 40:31). Those who entwine their hearts with God's heart will find their souls and their soles in step together. We need balance. To paraphrase, and now these three remain: loving, abiding, and serving. But the greatest of these, with respect to burnout, is abiding.

Chapter 17
Coping with Failure

❧

Have I got news for you.

Failure is ubiquitous. Everyone—including you and I—will at one time or another feel its sinking sensation. Many, in fact, will come to know it well and often.

Have I just made your day? Mine neither, but there is good news just around the corner. To appreciate it, however, we need to look closer at this all-encompassing phenomenon of failure.

First, its contexts vary. You may fail in finances, following your government's lead in spending more money than you make. Do you ever confuse need with greed or risk too much for a wishful return?

I may fail in the workplace, getting an unsatisfactory performance evaluation or worse, getting a pink slip or its equivalent. Your jovial golfing buddy may be a mess in his job, but covering it so cleverly that his coworkers are not aware of his problem.

Our failure may relate to relationships: a personality clash at work, an estranged child at home, a divorce. Power struggles also occur at church, for relational failure is always involved when Christians do battle with each other.

Failure may touch our fulfillment factor. Deferred gratification in personal fulfillment may, during the waiting period between vision and reality, be fertile soil for feelings of failure. Denied gratification, even more so.

Second, its consequences can be negative. How did you feel the last time you failed in some area of life?

There can be deep inner turmoil, fear, anger or rejection. You may feel a profound, though camouflaged, loss of self-esteem, or sense a loss of others' respect. Failure does seem to reveal your real friends, doesn't it?

You might have an unenviable encounter with a self-righteous do-gooder who sidles over to you and, looking intently into your eyes, says, "There must be sin in your life, or this wouldn't have happened." You may become a gnarled, grouchy pessimist. Or a gnarled, grouchy, bitter pessimist.

Third, its causes are several. Sometimes we have to honestly admit that we gave it poor effort. We simply did not put ourselves into that assignment or relationship.

Other times failure comes from poor discipline. Again, we do ourselves no favors by avoiding reality. If it is true that we botched a job or a relationship through some lack of self-control, we need to accept responsibility and move onward with life, humbler and wiser.

On the other hand, sometimes a perceived failure is actually just a poor fit. In these instances, we gain no virtue in blaming ourselves masochistically. If Jane gets an unsatisfactory performance review, it may simply confirm that she is not "wired" to do that particular work.

The problem then is not with Jane, but with the way she was selected for that position. (We discussed the Peter Principle and other pervasive practices in chapter 15.)

Benefits of Failure

Lest our focus on failure be overwhelming about now, let me hasten to a welcome consolation: Failure is the back door to success.

What? How?

Failure teaches us about ourselves. An interesting book about this is *When Smart People Fail*.[19] Taking a secular-but-sane look at various people who went through "job failure," the authors show how the experience helped various individuals refocus their careers in directions more aligned with the people they discovered themselves to be.

The draftsman may discover, when "released" from his job for being too avant-garde, that he is a hit in art advertising. The corporate executive, cooped up in a politics-bound headquarters office until a merger ousts her from the nest, may find a rekindled sparkle back in her eyes as an entrepreneur in a related business sector.

Neither may have made that discovery without the precipitating failure and the self-awareness it generated as they tried to understand what happened. I, myself, have a little personal experience in this pilgrimage.

My earlier career revolved around music and ministry. To combine these challenging, interesting, multifaceted arenas into one position, minister of worship, was wonderful. It required that I wear two hats, one as a pastor and another as chief musician. Both required a servant-leadership style. I welcomed the challenge and worked hard to earn the right for each. I studied music intently, earning undergraduate and graduate degrees and receiving encouraging kudos along the way.

My preparation for the pastorate included a rigorous academic program in Bible and related studies. Several years after graduation and after further preparation, I was ordained as a pastor, confirming my commitment to ministry.

I prayed with my people, played with them, comforted them, confronted them, counseled them, was blessed by them and sought to be a blessing to them in return. They knew that I cared for them as one of their pastors, not as their resident Christian recording/performing guru.

I avidly studied effective leadership and tried to practice it faithfully. I was thrilled to see leaders, relationships and programs develop in my sphere of ministry. I taught church music leadership in college and in professional seminars.

With all this training, all this experience, and all these relationships, how could I be dismissed from church leadership? How could I be told I didn't fit there? Easily, it turns out! And beneficially, it turned out. But how did I cope at the time, you ask?

Let me be quite honest. Lifestyle worship notwithstanding, the experience was not a joyride. Winter may have its moments of beauty, but it is not a thrill.

I felt the cold, and it penetrated my bark. I rehearsed gnawing questions of what I might have done wrong that precipitated my dismissal. Concern that Satan could use the situation to stir up dissension in our church led Jan and me to withhold the sharing of our griefs, questions, and concerns with friends in church. That, in turn, led to concern about hurting friends if they misunderstood our nondisclosure of the details behind our departure. A catch-22.

Added to that, of course, was daily rejection in the marketplace as I searched for work, the suspicious looks ("Why does that guy want this job?"), the hurt, the sense of betrayal. I found myself slowly sinking into the quicksand of a sense of worthlessness.

I seldom felt any inner exultation. I was mostly numb. It was a classic time for faith. Perceptions in such moments may not be reliable, but the feelings that come with the perceptions are nevertheless real. I have to say honestly that we're talking deep winter here. We're talking deep, bleak winter.

Failing Successfully

What about its cures? How can we cope successfully with failure?

If some sort of failure is a fact of life, then our lifestyle of worship needs to accommodate it. Good news: It does!

Let's put failure in perspective. Failure is an experience, not a trait.

Not all may agree on whether or not a particular experience is to be considered a nonsuccess. It's a matter of perception, which at times can be very subjective. Our world system's perception of failure, for example, can differ significantly from God's perception as we observe it in Scripture. The world says, "Don't throw away your life in some obscure jungle, swatting mosquitoes with a bunch of stone-age natives. You have an interesting, lucrative career here. Don't quit it!"

The counsel of friends, relatives and significant others, which emerge from their perceptions, may or may not be wise. Listen discerningly! Sylvia Nash, current CEO of the Christian Management Association, related these interesting bits of biographical data in a recent speech:

Beethoven's music teacher said, "As a composer, he is hopeless."

A music teacher told Caruso, "You can't sing. You have no voice at all."

Walt Disney was fired by a newspaper editor who decided that Walt had no good ideas.

Einstein could not speak until he was four years old and did not read until he was seven.

In acting school, Lucille Ball was told by her teacher that she would never amount to anything as an actress.

As a youngster, Thomas Edison's teachers said he was stupid.

Moses, you recall, was also vastly underrated, dismissed by some of his future followers as a muddling, meddling murderer. Joseph was sold for cash by his brothers. David was the last son Jesse expected Samuel to anoint as the future king.

We can all take comfort in the realization that sometimes even those close to us underestimate our capacity. Are there people in your life right now who have "written you off," who don't seem to see beyond the setback to the possiblity that your setback may have freed you for a much more fulfilling career? Are you letting them limit your perspective?

Whether the failure you have in mind as you read these pages is a problem of perception or "the real thing," the fact remains that it can help move you toward success. The setback can still be a step forward in lifetime effectiveness.

You may find that it causes you to reconsider your motives. Honestly done, that can be an amazing eye-opener. It may lead you to reexamine your abilities. Or your attitudes. Good move!

Could it be that letting go of that lesser goal (albeit unwillingly) may be part of the process of achieving a higher goal?

Strategy for Coping

From that perspective let's develop a plan.

First, since God is in control, your response is more important than your circumstance. The apostle Paul was put in prison. What happened? He witnessed to everyone within earshot, and the Gospel for which he was imprisoned moved forward unabated (Phil. 1). Prior to sacrificing his life, his word to the Philippian church was, of all things, "Rejoice" (Phil. 4:4). *Rejoice* is a meaningful word: "Return to the source of your joy." Wow, what that return can heal! What a dwelling place for our minds.

Second, since God is in control, your assignment is to abide. Obey the exhortation of James (James 1); follow the example of Job (Job 1). Will you let your experience make you *bitter* or *better?* The difference is one letter. You can focus on *I* (self) or on *E* (Emmanuel—God with us). Remember Hannah?

Talk and listen to God. He cares even about the details of your life. Bobby Jackson, a Christian friend who coaches in the NFL, discovered an interesting quote that certainly applies to the worship of abiding as we recover from a failure: "When you are sick at heart, talk it over with the great Physician. No appointment necessary!"

Remain in His Word. My lifeline was the book of Psalms. David came to my rescue time after time. Often he began his psalms with outbursts expressing the dismay, alarm or discouragement I felt. By the time he was finished, though, he looked to God and acknowledged Him as the Person on the other end of his and my lifeline.

God used these psalms to lift my eyes from my engulfing circumstances to His almighty sovereignty (see Ps. 121).

Remain with His children. Fellowship at such times is very important. Other godly believers become an irreplaceable support group.

While Jan and I deliberately kept silent concerning the circumstances surrounding my resignation, we continued meeting and associating with church friends at least weekly. Their friendship meant so much to us! True friends that they were, they understood and respected our silence without resorting to gossip or dissension.

Third, put feet to your faith. Work yourself (1 Cor. 10:31). The Bible makes some very uncomplimentary remarks about sluggards. Put your heart into your work, your relationships, your family responsibilities. Do it as an act of worship.

Control yourself (1 Cor. 9:24-27). Pilgrim's pathway is littered with the lives of compromised Christians, big fish and little ones. Watch out for the roaring lion, who devours victims one bite at a time (1 Peter 5:8).

Know yourself (Rom. 12:3-8). Determine to operate from strength. Life is too short for us to spend substantial time improving what we don't enjoy and don't do well. Instead, let's spend our time improving what we *do* enjoy and *do* do well. Don't use this as an excuse, however, to avoid the less welcome aspects of a well-fitting job. All work has its warts!

Failure is a bridge to better abiding and to more effective serving. What does God want to accomplish through your past failure?

Chapter 18

Making a Difference

🍂

I don't want to simply make a living. Any pagan can do that. I want to make a difference," the note read.

The cry of a hurting heart, it was a combined expression of frustration and commitment. I had first written that note to myself as I searched for work. I later reiterated it when I found work and sought to make it more than a mere source of income.

As I looked at lives in the marketplace, I saw some who seemed significant, in small or salient ways. Others—regardless of rank or income level—seemed trapped into simply making a living, earning a paycheck, hanging on until retirement rescued them. My soul ached for assurance that God had not put me aside. I yearned to once again sense worthwhileness in my work.

Have you ever felt this way?

How can we rise above the mundane routines of work—whether as an executive, a student, a homemaker or a sales clerk—and really make a difference?

What, for that matter, does it mean to "make a difference"? How do we know when we've done it?

Let's begin with the last two questions, then move up the list. We make a difference when our action or interaction results in a positive change. This can be any change within our sphere of influence: an improvement in mind-set (our own or someone else's), attitude, perspective, morale, etc.; in effectiveness, of our work or someone else's; and/or in relationships.

As you look at some of the areas in which you can make a difference in your marketplace, I must caution you to watch out: It can be fun.

You may have the opportunity to make a work-effectiveness difference. Your specific influence, for example, may be in your company's efficiency, design, training, organization, sales, marketing, budgeting, accounting, purchasing, analysis or quality control. Any aspect of the work in which you find yourself is fair game for improvement.

Are you still with me? Let's take a moment to pause for perspective. Why do this for your company? To get a raise? For a promotion?

Those may result from your work, but with your worship lenses on, you see this job as an opportunity to please your real Boss, your Father in heaven. He is the reason you give it your best shot. He is the reason you want your presence in that position to make a difference.

Whenever you have an appropriate opportunity to make a difference, big or small, just do it. Do it for the fun of it, for the improvement of it, and as a way of worship.

Make Paul's words come alive: "Whatever you do, do it all for the glory of God" (1 Cor. 10:31).

At times we are not even aware that we are making a difference. On one hand, we may work diligently but not see any results. Missionaries in various cultures and prayer warriors know this feeling well. On the other hand, we may unknowingly influence others as we simply go about our daily life and activity. We parents, sometimes to our amazement and other times to our chagrin, discover how closely—and covertly—our children have watched and copied our key attitudes, behaviors, and values.

Influence happens at almost any age, though. I vividly recall God's encouragement to me through another person as a college student. One day as I walked across campus on my way to class, a fellow student interrupted my lofty thoughts.

"You don't know me," he began, "but I remember you from high school!"

"You went to Bell High?" I asked. High school seemed a long way back, since in the interim I had graduated from one institution and, after changing majors, was now an upperclassman at this college. The guy had good recall, and good memories too, I hoped!

"I was a new student in one of the groups you took on an orientation tour of the school, just before my first semester began.

You were one of the first kids I met on campus, a senior, and a Christian, so I watched you during the year.

"I saw you in sports, in music, in drama, in club leadership and so on. I just want you to know that your example as a Christian in a secular high school was a real testimony to me. Thanks so much."

In less than a minute from the time he stopped me, he was gone. His brief comments, however, have remained with me for over twenty years. How thrilled I was that he had caught me in the act of doing something right.

We can only imagine how many people we may have affected, positively and negatively, over the years. Perhaps you can get an idea of the scope of your influence by thinking back to those who have made big and little differences in your life. Sobering, isn't it?

That's what you can do in your marketplace, as worship.

How? Let It Flow!

How do we go about "making a difference"? How do we interact positively with our world, our sphere of influence?

We focus on loving Him, abiding in Him, and serving Him. The rest flows from that core. "Whoever believes in Me, as the Scripture has said, streams of living water will flow from within him" (John 7:38).

If we make our worship of Him a lifestyle, we can expect certain general effects. If we focus on loving, abiding and serving, a comprehensive list is neither possible nor necessary.

One expression, as we noted in chapter 15, is a goodness of fit between our design and our work. This is both a platform for personal significance and an example to others which may stimulate them to live in harmony with God's design of them.

A true worshiper will work wholeheartedly. Remember 1 Corinthians 10:31? This makes a difference in the quality of work accomplished and again sets an example for others.

A true worshiper will lift others up. "Be devoted to one another in brotherly love. Honor one another above yourselves" (Rom. 12:10). This may be normal at home, but it is rather countercultural at work.

We are the "Me" generation. We are told that to be successful we need to lift ourselves up, to toot our own horn. There is a kernel of truth there: As part of your "sober judgment" of yourself, you need to know your strengths. As part of your work evaluation, your boss needs to know what you have accomplished. As part of your organizational review, the board needs to know what right things have been done.

Beyond that, however, your problem with lifting others up may be your fear that they will somehow be seen as superior to you. If you lift them up, won't that put you down?

First answer this question: If Millie routinely criticizes those around her, how does that affect your impression of her? Often it backfires. When we constantly put others down, we go down also—or instead.

Basically, the issue is selfishness. We withhold praise from others because it threatens us. It may take something we want away from us. Selfishness is sin.

If you commit this area to God in worship, you will risk lifting others up. Why? Because God is sovereign.

You can glorify Him in His sovereignty by trusting His sovereignty more. If He wants you in that position or at that income level—and if you are loving, abiding and serving—you will have that position or income. Therefore, if you trust Him, you can afford to lift others up without having to feel threatened or jealous. It's positively liberating!

Attitudes make a difference also. Your worshiping attitude toward God affects your attitude toward yourself, toward others, and toward your work. Your attitudes affect others too, for better or for worse.

A thankful heart implies a thoughtful heart. What kind of thoughts should fill our hearts? Paul gives a countercultural answer: "Finally, brothers, whatever is true, whatever is noble, whatever is right, whatever is pure, whatever is lovely, whatever is admirable—if anything is excellent or praiseworthy—think about such things" (Phil. 4:8).

These thoughts can fill your heart with thanksgiving to God and make a profound difference, given their dramatic contrast to the preoccupation of today's media with violence, anger, revenge, immorality, etc.

Part of our worship is the disciplining of our thought habits. Isn't it wonderful that God can renew our minds!

A good summary of the marketplace difference lifestyle worship makes can be seen in the qualities God wants in church leadership. Paul's letters to Titus and Timothy list leadership criteria, from which the following are excerpted: above reproach, temperate, prudent, respectable, hospitable, gentle, uncontentious, free from the love of money, self-controlled, loving what is good (see Titus 1:5-9 and 1 Tim. 3:1-13).

Forgiving One Another

Is there room in your marketplace for forgiveness? Romans 12 closes with an entire section (vv. 17-21) about forgiveness. Why so many verses (plus others elsewhere) on one basic theme? You're right: Because God knows our lower nature.

As we close this chapter on making a difference, let's consider how we can do ourselves a favor, and those around us. Let's ponder the grace of forgiveness as an act of worship.

Once upon a time, in a cozy little neighborhood of a comfortable little town, two young families lived next door to each other. Each family had children of about the same ages who grew up together from babyhood through high school.

Billy and Teddy were inseparable buddies. From the time they were put into the same crib as their moms met for coffee, they played together, laughed together, got into trouble together, went places together, and giggled about girls together.

Years passed, and the boys graduated from high school. Bill and Ted worked in the same store in town. They drove to and from work together. After work, they still played together, laughed together, helped each other, and talked about young women together.

Eventually, they married the ladies on whom their most earnest conversations were centered. Each participated in the other's wedding, and they continued to play together, laugh together, help each other, drive to work together, and talk together about marriage and children.

With the passing of years came the premature passing of Ted's wife. Bill's friendship and support were special comforts to Ted during that difficult time.

They laughed together over happy memories they had created as a foursome. They cried together over the profound loss and coming changes. And as before Ted's wife's death, they continued to play together, help each other, drive to work together, and enjoy each other's company.

Time brought more changes. Bill's health failed dramatically. Hit severely with disease, it was a marvel that he continued to live.

Each now had suffered a key loss: Ted had lost his wife and Bill had lost his health. Yet they still laughed together and enjoyed each other's company.

As Bill's medical problems mushroomed, something else developed as well. Ted had always found Bill's wife attractive. Widowed now, he was increasingly interested in her.

Bill had been aware of Ted's passive interest in Sharon for years and was not particularly concerned. It was, in fact, a compliment to his own good judgment that his buddy found his wife such a desirable person.

One evening after the three had enjoyed dinner together, Bill excused himself from the table to go into the kitchen. While Bill was in the kitchen, Ted, in the next room, made some very personal suggestions to Sharon. What neither knew was that Bill overheard the conversation.

Shocked, sickened, and profoundly violated by his best friend, Bill waited what seemed like an eternity before trusting himself to reenter the room. From that night onward he internalized his anger, saying nothing but carrying a deep pain.

Nothing came of Ted's comments, thanks to Sharon's integrity. However, the warm relationship between the two men cooled noticeably. Their laughter became formal, their kindred spirit was gone and get-togethers became strained as others sensed Bill's coldness to Ted.

Bill explained himself to no one. Suspecting that Ted would pass off this incident superficially, and being a person who generally avoids confrontations anyway, Bill didn't even confront Ted with his knowledge of that overheard conversation.

The result, inside Bill, was years of simmering anger and unresolved bitterness, a result which was no help at all to his increasing health problems.

Bill was a Christian. He loved and served God enthusiastically. He knew that he should forgive his friend, but he felt incapable of doing so. This dilemma was a constant struggle and burden.

More years passed. More changes came. Both men retired. Sharon died.

Some things did not change. The unforgiveness survived Sharon's death. The former buddies still no longer laughed together, no longer helped each other, no longer went places together. Ted's health was fine; Bill was getting more and more feeble.

Time carved another benchmark: Bill had to move into a convalescent care center. Too weak to walk, he was constantly confined either to bed or to a wheelchair.

His head drooped. He could hardly lift his hand to feed himself. You wouldn't have recognized him from the back, and he looked 199 years old from the front.

One day, along with several other friends, Ted came to visit Bill. For about an hour, everyone chatted cordially. To the surprise of several in the room, the visit was a genuinely pleasant and heart-warming experience!

Bill's attitude toward Ted had changed 180 degrees. The difference escaped no one, and the atmosphere took on characteristics not enjoyed for well over a decade.

Finally it was time for the visit to end. Each person hugged Bill, said good bye, and filed out of his room.

Ted was the last to leave. When the room was empty except for the two lifelong friends, they began to talk quietly and earnestly.

Tears came to both sets of aging eyes. Then smiles to both faces. Then came the laughter, just like old times. Finally the reunited buddies embraced each other, and Ted left Bill's room.

One week later, Bill died.

His final, great act of worship was to sacrifice the bitterness and anger he harbored and replace those emotional malignancies with forgiveness.

Without excusing Ted's obvious offense, think about Bill's response. Did bitterness make him better? No. More likely, the reverse is true.

Did his anger help anything? No. It worked against him, affecting him and those around them negatively. Unforgiveness is costly.

Forgiveness can be tough, at times almost impossible. However, when forgiveness is most difficult to extend, then it is most necessary to extend.

Thank God that He gave us the Holy Spirit! It is God in us Who helps us do the otherwise impossible.

God knows all about forgiveness. He created it, models it, and commands it for our own good, for the good of those around us, and for His glory: "Get rid of all bitterness, rage and anger. . . . Be kind and compassionate to one another, forgiving each other, just as in Christ God forgave you" (Eph. 4:31-32).

Chapter 19

Managing to Worship

❦

Dan was a person with a future. Bright, handsome, articulate, ambitious, eager to serve God, he had everything it took to achieve his goals.

Even as a college underclassman, he knew what career he wanted—join a particular national parachurch organization; he knew what organization he wanted to belong to—hereinafter called The Group; and he knew what position he wanted to attain—president. With this single focus, he devoted himself to jumping through the necessary hoops to achieve his goals.

First, he graduated from college; then he was accepted into The Group. For almost a decade, he served in various parts of the country, moving from newcomer to veteran within The Group.

The Group leadership took notice and invited Dan to remain at headquarters and serve in the general administration of The Group. Dan was given one area of responsibility, then another and another. Each required managerial skills and each was progressively nearer "the corner office."

However, over a period of time leaders within The Group discovered a disturbing pattern emerging. Dan cut a wide swath, but in his wake were the corpses of other people who had somehow gotten in his way.

Under his ambition was a pride that tolerated no opposition. Getting on Dan's bad side was a big mistake. Those he couldn't manipulate found themselves transferred to some other region of the country.

It is not that he was totally self-serving. Some in The Group were devoted to him because of his help at one crucial time or another.

Others, however, carried their self-esteem away in a sling after he was done with them.

Other problems surfaced as well: wrong people put into key slots, interpersonal conflicts he chose to ignore, and counsel on these concerns from the leaders unheeded by Dan.

Sensing finally that things were not going according to plan, Dan began to withdraw from others. Eventually he retreated to a memo-writing and number-crunching management mode, leaving his office only for must-do meetings of one kind or another.

His next responsibility was a 3-D (Definite Dip Downward). One year later, after twenty years of service and a widely circulated parting shot at leadership for "not supporting him," Dan left The Group, moved far away and took employment in a completely unrelated field.

What happened? Didn't he "have it"? Was he burned out? Was the Peter Principle in action again?

No such situation is single-faceted. A major contributing factor, though, was his lack of worship-filled management.

That's not a common diagnosis, is it? Worship-filled management: Is it a new buzz term in the industry? Though not intended to be trendy, we all would gain if it became a trend.

What is it? How can we do it? Is this a new style of management? Good questions!

Worship-filled management is more foundational than style. Underneath such variables as personality and situation which may influence your management style to be democratic or participatory, worship-filled management addresses your very motivation.

Do you genuinely want God to be glorified in the way you manage? Have you ever wondered how to make that happen?

A look at a typical organization will help us appreciate the importance of managers. Most organizations are comprised broadly of three personnel categories: leadership, management, and staff. Leaders conceptualize and communicate the vision of the organization. They look ahead, design a way to match mission with need, set the course, muster support, and ignite the staff.

Staff, paid and/or volunteer, actually get the work done. They are gifted in myriads of ways needed to accomplish the organizational mission.

Between leadership and staff is a big chasm—the canyon between vision and reality. If the organization is simply well-led, the charisma of the leadership will attract good people on board the ship. Once aboard, though, if no one tells them what to do, where to do it, how to interface, how they will be measured, where the stuff is—high turnover results as unfulfilled people realize that working there is not working out.

Managers step into that gap. They have the crucial, dual responsibilities of developing and maintaining structure while also developing and maintaining people.

As a lifestyle worshiper in a managerial role, you can look at this organizational process through worship lenses. Given that you and those you manage are designed for worship, this is a triple-win approach: You win, your managees win, and God wins. It's best for all involved. What a privilege to have this responsibility and to shoulder it in a way that honors God!

The "heavy" side of this privilege is that a manager is not only to be a good steward of his or her own life as an act of worship, but also of the working lives of those reporting to him or her. Ouch!

Conceptually, we will become the best managers we can be when we habitually see both the privileges and responsibilities of our position through God's eyes and then fulfill the role in His way.

Practically, what differences might an observer note when our management becomes part of our lifestyle worship? Let's begin with ourselves.

Managing Ourselves

First is personal integrity. We will walk our talk. Following sixteen verses of specifics (Eph. 4:17-32), Paul lays down a clear challenge: "Be imitators of God, therefore, as dearly loved children and live a life of love, just as Christ loved us and gave himself up for us as a fragrant offering and sacrifice to God" (Eph. 5:1-2).

At the core is love. Emerging from that love, personal integrity is part of the worship of abiding. Before we can serve worshipfully as managers, we need thus to be constantly renewed in the spirit of our mind (Eph. 4:23). Only when accompanied with the right kind of loving and abiding will our serving be fruitful as God desires (see John 15).

Second is servant leadership. We also see in Ephesians 5:2 that God's call is to servant leadership. Service is hot; self-service is not! As Christ did on a major scale, we in a small way may find it wise to empty ourselves as managers of this "right" or that privilege in order to accomplish something greater. We need to remember that God's ultimate glory is more important than our immediate comfort. And that is definitely counter-cultural.

Third is vision. We will see the whole picture that the leadership sees—not just our own slice of the pie. Managers often compete with each other for bigger budget shares or better equipment.

In contrast, we will look at everything and see how our part fits the whole and how limited resources should be apportioned throughout the organization so as to maximize its long-range effectiveness. That is, we'll help leadership do the right things— even if it means that our department gets diminished in the best interests of the overall organization.

And a corollary to this: We won't let the tail wag the dog, even if we're the tail. We will do things right, within our department and within the organization as a whole.

Fourth is priorities. People are more important than projects. That's a hard truth. But we are to be imitators of God, right?

The first perfect happening on earth was creation. God did it. The last was Christ's sacrifice for our sins. God did that too.

You probably cannot think of a project between or since that hasn't been a compromise. Why? Because of people. Why does God let it happen time after time? Because to Him, people are more important than projects.

Years ago, a good friend of mine accepted an invitation to become the senior pastor of a large church. Until this time, he had been an associate pastor of a few mid-sized congregations, so this was a major move.

Before leaving the church he then served as an associate minister, he asked a few members what advice they had for him as he began this new stage and new setting. He told me about the priceless input of one person: "Sometimes I get the feeling that you are walking right past people on your way to another project."

My friend remembered that advice. The church he now pastors has absolutely flourished under his care over the last several years.

How many times have you seen or heard of a project that was snarled up in problems while the people involved were sorting out theirs? A building stands unfinished because there was not genuine agreement to support it when construction began . . . a body splits because believers disagree over whether to have drums in the church service . . . a people starves to death while mission agencies compete over who's going to have control.

People are more important than projects. Take care of the people first. Then, it's amazing how quickly the projects are taken care of as well.

Fifth is problems. Managers face one problem after another. That sounds like bad news, but just as flying an airplane is a process of making constant corrections to keep it flying in the right direction at the right altitude and speed, management is a process of making constant corrections. There's a sense in which managers can be thankful for problems—that's why they are needed!

Worship-filled management is as realistic as it is heavenly. As Nehemiah, we will anticipate problems where possible and prepare alternatives as part of our planning process. Nehemiah's example—not only of rebuilding a city wall, but of rebuilding a people—is a very profitable study.

Like Jehoshaphat, we can meet problems without panic, not because we always know what to do but because we know Whom to keep our eyes on. In their unique ways, both men show the worship of putting feet to faith.

Sixth is prayer. Both Jehoshaphat and Nehemiah, not so incidentally, were men of prayer. Prayer was an integral part of their worship of abiding, and neither was even a minister. Pick a quiet place and an unhurried moment, then read 2 Chronicles 20 and the book of Nehemiah, noting each man's constant communion with God. What examples they are of lifestyle worship!

Seventh is mentoring. If you have been in management for awhile, you have collected significant experience. Wouldn't you have been thrilled if another, more experienced manager had shared experiences, insights, and contacts with you early in your career?

Why not share yourself with another Christian up-and-comer in the spirit of 2 Timothy 2:2? Whether in your organization or another, you can help prepare that person for effective ministry through management. It's another way of giving yourself, of extending your influence, of worshiping.

Eighth is time. Management soaks up time like a dry sponge soaks up water. Like motherhood, like management: The work never ends.

Occasionally, long hours are unavoidable. However, when we fall into the trap of constantly working long weeks, we kid ourselves if we think it will solve much. What often happens instead is that we slow down, become less creative, and less productive. But it's a great way to impress others who don't know better: friends, family, the boss. My, what we won't do to ourselves for a little sense of significance.

We traditionally think of a full-time work week as about forty hours. Many executives and sales professionals, however, work sixty to eighty hours per week as a matter of habit.

Think about it: A sixty-hour week is the equivalent of working Monday through Friday from 8 A.M. to 8 P.M., not counting the commute. Say good-bye to family time until about noon on Saturday.

A fifty-six-hour week is the equivalent of working eight hours per day, Sunday through Saturday. Not much rest in that schedule.

Even a forty-eight-hour week, which sounds like vacation compared to a sixty-hour week, is the equivalent of working eight hours a day Monday through Saturday. Yet, how much time does it leave for family, routine chores, casual get-togethers, and personal renewal?

I spend lots of time with elderly people, some enjoying retirement and others on their death bed. Not once in years have I heard any of them say, "I wish I had spent more time at the office." More often, it is the reverse.

Lifestyle worship demands that we manage our time. One way to do so is to control our work, rather than allow it to control us. We really are less crucial to our organization than our egos often lead us to believe. Appropriate time away from work, in fact, can bring us back more refreshed and productive than if we had stayed longer or brought home a bulging briefcase.

My own schedule is a little crazy. Some work weeks, particularly when I am out of town, are sixty-plus hours long. I feel the difference keenly, since listening is an important part of my work and I don't listen well when fatigued.

I keep track of time. Then I try to compensate for long weeks by giving more time either beforehand or afterward to enjoyable exercise with friends or to other productive-but-not-work-related activity.

An average work week of about forty-five hours enables me to maintain a sense of balance and productivity. It also keeps me from being swallowed by my work, which I happen to enjoy.

What are you doing to control your time?

Managing Others

The staff you manage is made up of some very special people. Do you know them? Really know them?

The author of Hebrews advised: "Consider how we may spur one another on toward love and good deeds. . ." (Heb. 10:24). Isn't that what people management is all about? Let's consider some areas of people contact with worship in mind.

First is recruitment. To be imitators of Christ in this area may be a bit uncomfortable. Why Jesus chose whom He did as disciples, for example, is a total mystery. Look at their résumés—and He wanted to build His church on this motley crew? He did it, and with them.

By way of application, sometimes your best recruits will be the least obvious. Look beyond the résumé to the person's history of joy, success, and interests. A person with the approved experience may not be nearly as effective as one with a heart for what needs to be done.

Second is communication. Communicate freely, and as fully as appropriate. This includes confronting with gentleness (Gal. 6:1). Don't duck it, but do it right.

It includes challenging, "stimulating" one another to love and good works (Heb. 10:24). That term is from "paroxysm," like the friction between a match and a rough surface to spark the flame. The word is used to describe the argument over John Mark that split Paul and Barnabas from one group into two.

This is no wimpy challenge. However, some people need this kind of confrontation on occasion. More often, less volatile conversations will do just fine!

Communicating is encouraging one another (Heb. 10:25). A well-placed and sincere word of encouragement can do wonders for morale and effort. But you already know that, I'm sure.

Third is support. Commit yourself to building relationships which enable you to get to know your staff. This is not necessarily a buddy-buddy friendship; it can be very professional, if that is the context in which you work.

The purpose—no more, no less—is twofold. First, you help them discover how God designed them. Second, you help them take appropriate steps to develop the areas in which you and they sense God wants them to grow professionally. How? Tests, seminars, encouragement, opportunity. You are a steward; you can figure out how to get it done in your context and budget.

"Sure," you say. "I'll help them discover and develop their gifts. Then they'll leave us. Or, worse, take my place. Or—horror of horrors—become my boss. Great idea."

Risk it. If God designed that person for such a role—no matter what the role—who are you to stand in the way?

In fact, would you even truly want to be an obstacle to God's development of that person? How much more fulfilling—fun, even—to be part of His plan for that person.

Do your folks a favor: Plant them where they are gifted, not simply where you need a slot filled. Chapter 15, "Fulfilling Your Call" enlarges on this, so you may wish to reread it from a manager's viewpoint.

Fourth is to create an antiburnout environment. Another favor you can do your folks—and yourself—is reread chapter 16, "Burning Out for God," with your manager's hat on. Anything you can do to keep your staff in refreshed balance will lower your turnover and raise your effectiveness—two effects which will do you no disfavor personally or professionally.

Fifth is evaluation. We all need feedback about our work. Most performance reviews relate the person to the task. How do you measure your staff? How do they measure you?

With all that has been said above in mind, let me make two brief suggestions which I heard first from Dr. Ted Engstrom, president emeritus of World Vision. First, modify your evaluation process, so that you relate the performance to the task—and the person to his or her potential. What a difference that change makes!

Second, evaluate upward as well as downward. Get input from the staff you supervise on how well they think you're doing. That may sound daring, but if you have the personal integrity not to hold their "suggestions" against them, what better opportunity can you have to enhance relationships and performance than in a mutually accountable setting?

I've done this, and sometimes it's humbling. Of course, that is when it is most needed. It also affirms, reinforcing the moments people have caught me in the act of doing something right.

All things considered, and done in the right spirit, this upward evaluation is a very beneficial way to embody servant leadership. It's another triple-win situation.

Et cetera. We haven't addressed such other relationships as those with sales prospects, vendors, our own boss (every manager has at least one), or other organizations. However, if we can even bat .667 on what we did address, we'll have no problem applying lifestyle worship to these other situations.

May your management be an "I love You!" to God.

Chapter 20
Living It at Home

I remember seeing her walk into the choir rehearsal room. Accompanied by a couple of friends with whom she talked animatedly, she went over to the music rack and slipped her choir folder out of its slot.

She didn't take one look in my direction. That gave me, seated on the other side of the room, a great opportunity to gaze unself-consciously at her.

"I'd like to get to know that girl better," I thought to myself. Over the next year, I did. Two years after meeting her, we were engaged.

My proposal for marriage was a little out of the ordinary: I didn't do it in person! During the summer prior to my senior year in college, I flew little airplanes just outside Chicago, training for what I thought would be a career in missionary aviation.

Jan was on her way to the British Isles with the choir to which we both belonged. The idea of Jan spending several weeks on tour with my carnivorous Christian college comrades was unsettling to me. I knew their dark hearts and I knew my fair maiden and I knew I needed to protect her from them.

One evening, after consulting with my father who happened to be in Chicago at the moment, I caught up with the choir by telephone. They were in New York that night. Calling Jan out of the preconcert meeting, I asked her to marry me. An eternal moment later, she accepted my proposal.

Now, a quarter of a century and three kids later, we're still friends and lovers. And, as anyone with marriage experience knows, that is much easier said than done. True for us, true for you, true for anyone who says, "I do."

As Partners

Marriage is a major lifetime adjustment. The first couple of years may seem like the time of biggest change, but the reality is that throughout life together, mates constantly adjust for circumstances and for each other. "In sickness and in health, for richer or for poorer . . ." is reality.

Marriage is like a ship going out to sea. Anyone setting sail knows buffeting will come, sometimes externally and other times internally.

About half of the marriages don't make it. They become shipwrecked; they crack up. Whether a problem of poor mate selection, half-hearted commitment, or sheer stupidity, any such shipwreck is a financial, emotional, and spiritual disaster. We all have many dear personal friends whose marriages have come apart, and all have been deeply affected by its ravage and pain.

An ideal marriage is—of all things—a love triangle. In one corner is the wife; in the other, her husband. At the apex of the triangle is God Himself. The closer our communion which is expressed in loving and abiding, with God, the closer our communion with each other.

Does this mean that every marital problem has a spiritual solution? Human relationships are not quite that simplistic.

It does mean, however, that if you and your mate allow lifestyle worship to permeate your marriage, you will save yourselves a lot of grief and anxiety and give yourselves a lot of joy and peace. And God will be glorified in you. Many marriages are already a triangle. God is not at the apex, however. Instead, the third party may be money. Or career(s). Or golf. Or another person.

When we exchange marriage vows, we vow a lifetime of mutual commitment. Nowhere else on earth is there an agreement quite like marriage vows. These vows are binding, and that is why they are so serious.

Why are vows even necessary, when two people are "so in love"? Because such commitment is contrary to our evil nature. We tend to veer off-course, as God points out time after time in Scripture and as Israel demonstrates repeatedly in the Bible. That is why vows are so necessary.

Part of our worship, then, is to make our marriage a living example of what God wants it to be. That's tough—but if it were easy, it would be no big deal, right?

God makes it a big deal. He even compares what He wants to see in our marriages with Christ's relationship to the church, instructing us to be like-minded (Eph. 5:22-23). The mandate is inescapable—and what a standard!

Jan and I are stewards, managers really, of our relationship. We each belong to Him, not ourselves. "You are not your own; you were bought at a price. Therefore honor God" (1 Cor. 6:19-20).

Likewise, our relationship belongs to Him as part of our Romans 12:1 sacrifice to Him of all that we are and have. We have only this moment of management responsibility. When we get to heaven, our stewardship will be over and we will return to Him "unattached," even though we'll continue to love each other.

If you are married, you too have only this moment. How are you handling it?

While marriage is our most important human relationship, we unfortunately often give more attention and nurture to occupational relationships (sales prospects, bosses, employees, colleagues, our career track), hobbies (golf lessons, tennis camps, arts & crafts classes) and home maintenance (front yards, furniture, decorating, do-it-yourself projects).

It's the American way. And it's one of the reasons our careers and homes often outlast our marriages. What do you suppose would happen if we were evaluated on our management of our marriage relationship as we are on our jobs?

Have you ever heard someone say, "It's what you can't see that counts"? What we cannot materially see is more important than what we can. Relationships are more valuable than our visible environment. "Better a dry crust with peace and quiet than a house full of feasting, with strife" (Prov. 17:1).

One way we worship God in marriage is by honoring that relationship as He does, above other competing relationships and tangible attention-getters.

This is not just a commitment to continue the relationship; it is a commitment to nurture the relationship. Again, the word of God exhorts us to "live a life of love, just as Christ loved us and gave himself up for us as a fragrant offering and sacrifice to God" (Eph. 5:2).

How, you ask? Ephesians 5 presents some specifics. Looking at marriage as an illustration of our relationship with God, our lifestyle worship model offers a useful way of capturing the essence.

Love your mate with your heart, soul, and body. Let your mind dwell on your mate—not on someone else's—taking in whatever is lovely, whatever is praiseworthy, whatever is special. Let your heart be full of thanks to God for your mate; that tends to crowd out other harmful and competing thoughts.

Abide with your mate, looking to him or her for the nurture you need rather than looking elsewhere. Communicate freely and fully in ways that your mate understands and accepts. Trust your mate. Be trustworthy yourself.

Serve your friend and lover. Give of yourself to each other. Look out for each other. Help each other, not grudgingly or out of necessity, but out of desire.

This will be relatively easy in some marriages and almost impossible in others. But the model stands. God's mandate stands. And it's another "I love You!" to God.

As Parents

Children are special, that's for sure. Jan and I had no children for our first eight years of marriage, so when God finally sent them along, we were willing and ready. Our long wait sensitized us to couples who have not had kids, just as our experiences now with teenagers loose in the house sensitize us to others who do!

Raising kids is certainly an act of courage these days. Can it also be an act of worship? Count on it.

Again, it's the relationship that counts, not the income, not the address, not the toys, and not the clothes—although our kids may question at least the last of that litany. What matters most is their relationship with and worship of God: loving, abiding, serving.

Our principal role as parents is to manage—be stewards of—our children in a way that equips and facilitates their development of lifestyle worship that pleases and honors God. Everything else is secondary—everything else.

Managing children worshipfully, as crass as it sounds on first run, is similar to managing employees. Of course, it is much more intimate and grows from a much deeper love. Yet the similarities are there: train, encourage, confront, console, challenge, assign responsibilities as appropriate and as they are capable of fulfilling them, evaluate, correct, build their self-esteem, and so on.

As part of our worship, one of our delightful privileges and responsibilities is to see our children as the individuals God designed them to be. They are not each other, and they are not clones of their mom and dad. They are unique and wonderful creations, a little weird at times, but wonderful nonetheless.

For example, how do your children relate to others, alike or differently? We have fun with some of these analytical tools as a family and took one of the "social style" tests mentioned in chapter 15, "Fulfilling Your Call." We laughed at the way it revealed our differences!

Jan prefers a steadier, more methodical pace than the rest of us; I lean toward variety and unpredictability. Byron is comparatively reserved and intense, whereas Krista and Kara are very people-oriented and easygoing. We are all over the graph!

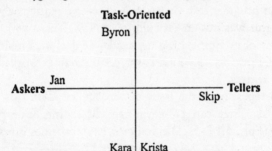

The Garmo family Personality Model

Several other interesting distinctions helped us not only see who we are but understand why we have some tense moments from time to time and how we can make it a little easier on each other.

It also influenced our expectations of each other: If we are designed differently, we should not expect each other to react or do everything as we do. And that, within parameters, is okay! That insight alone can be somewhat liberating.

Our best training tool for lifestyle worship is a good example. Just as children pick up their parents' anxieties, they can pick up on our worship—if we are consistent.

What are the elements of lifestyle worship?

- A loving heart. Do your kids sense your love for God and for people?
- An abiding spirit. If your trust is firmly in God, if your eyes are fixed on Him, if He is your source of spiritual nourishment, they'll know. And if He's not, they'll know.
- A serving mind-set. This is easy for them to observe, as well as your attitude in serving.

What does such modeling require? Time with the family, for one thing. Work demands and avocational demands need to be combatted continuously.

This came home to me while working on my doctorate. With a full-time job that regularly required extra hours, classes to attend once or twice a week, and a young family dashing through their early years of delightful living, I found that the only time for study was on my "day off" and evenings after the kids hit the sack.

This slowed my pace, and one result was that I "crowded" a three-year program into six years. Not being a particularly patient person, this was not an easy pill to swallow. Yet, it was the only way I saw of accomplishing my academic goal and maintaining the family priority to which I was committed. It worked, and I have no regrets.

Worth repeating is the issue of consistency. Our kids read us like books. They can be alarmingly discerning. Our personal integrity (Eph. 4:17–5:21) either crowns or crucifies our spiritual talk.

Time and integrity: A one-two combination that is tough to beat.

Helping your children understand their design can be a superb time of discovery and togetherness for you. What uniquenesses does she have in physical appearance and abilities? In what areas does he seem to be smartest and most interested? What are her personality strengths? What are his spiritual gifts?

Help them envision ways to use their particular design as an offering to God. Show them that there are several—perhaps many—ways God might use them, if they give themselves to Him.

Don't force them into your personal preference either overtly or subtly. Leading them is the Holy Spirit's privilege, not yours. (While they may move your way because of guilt or to please you, what you really want is for them to move His way because of commitment.)

Your kids will pay most attention to their flaws. Most of us do that to ourselves. Help them accept their design, with its pluses and minuses, thankfully from God. If they do, they are well on their way to glorifying God in their lives.

As they discover their design, another privilege of parenthood is to help them become as they are designed. Help them find and become involved with needs around them in ways that use and develop their giftedness. What a thrill to help fulfill their design!

In this area as well, your example will be very influential. Let them see you using your own giftedness with a thankful heart.

You may be tempted to list these ideas and force them into your world. Don't! This is not another list of rules to follow. These are anticipated results, expected outcomes, of your lifestyle worship. Don't worry about the how-tos. Just let them flow from your lifestyle. All you need remember is to love, abide and serve.

And teach your children to do likewise.

Chapter 21
Restoring Sunday to Sonday

Then I looked and heard the voice of many angels, number-
ing . . . ten thousand times ten thousand. They encircled
the throne and the living creatures and the elders. In a loud
voice they sang:
  "Worthy is the Lamb, who was slain,
  to receive power and wealth and wisdom
  and strength and honor and glory and praise!"
Then I heard every creature . . . singing:
  "To him who sits on the throne and to the Lamb
  be praise and honor and glory and power,
  for ever and ever!"
The four living creatures said, "Amen," and the elders fell
down and worshiped.   (Rev. 5:11-14)

Can you imagine what it will be like to witness such
worship when we all get to heaven? What a day of rejoicing that
will be!

In the meantime, how is your worship when you are with a group
of believers?

As I think of church worship, my mind goes back to childhood impressions. My early memories of worship services are
far different from the Revelation service you just read. Mine
could easily have become a series of Norman Rockwell scenes:
a cozy church, wooden pews (empty in front and crowded in
back), poor ventilation, long services, starched white shirts,

tight collars, itchy slacks, and grown-ups whose waists I barely reached.

And everywhere, gleaming smiles. It wasn't until later that I began to suspect some of those smiles were actually grimaces brought on by tight corsets and collars!

There was a comfortableness in the familiarity and predictability of it all. Everything fit into a cozy whole. Expectations of the members seemed to be fulfilled.

Years have passed and times have changed. Now we are members of a very large church. Pews are padded, temperature is perfect, and services are punctual. Starch is out, collars are in but open, my slacks don't itch, and I'm taller than most other adults.

Yet, some things have not changed at all. For many church attendees, there is a problem: no core. Even for genuine Christians, church can become just a wrapping of tightly woven activities and, for variety, another tightly woven list of things not to do.

Inside the wrapping there is nothing. "The worship service"— whatever form it takes, and the possibilities are legion—can become just another of these activities.

Do you ever "play church"?

At times this attitude is a reflection of the minister(s) up in front. Apart from using the term "worship" in reference to the Sunday morning meeting—other meeting times are also permitted, if your requisition is submitted in triplicate—they may give little or no attention to real worship. Shame on them!

More often it is our own distractedness. In that case, shame on us. We can do better.

But how? How can you and I restore Sunday to Sonday?

The Experience of Worship

Think sports for a moment; now, that is—not next Sunday morning. Pick a sport you enjoy playing. Any sport will do, but let's suppose that you are an enthusiastic tennis player.

Imagine this scenario: It's Monday. At 4:30 P.M., you dash out your office door to the car, rev it up and move it out to join the thundering herd heading homeward.

You, however, are going to make a lifestyle difference from the herd. You are going to stop for exercise on the way home.

As you navigate traffic, you're taking off your tie. At one stoplight, you slip off your black leather shoes. At the next one, on go the white tennis shoes.

By the time you swoop down into the tennis court parking lot going about forty-five mph), a metamorphosis has taken place. You're dressed like a lean, mean tennis pro!

But your mind is still back at the office. You jog over to the court, greet your partner, skip the warm-up, break out a new can of balls, elect to serve first, and begin the match immediately.

What happens to your game when you approach it this way? Disaster! Your feet are sluggish, your eyes are unfocused, and your mind is still wandering just like your tennis balls, which are spraying everywhere but between those little white lines.

Has your approach to corporate worship been at all similar to that? Determined to make a lifestyle difference, you dash to church for an hour or two on Sunday morning. Beforehand, you and your spouse have a mild lack of agreement. The kids, up late on Saturday night, are slow and cranky.

Late and agitated, you swoop into the church parking lot, run to church, try to resolve your spousal dispute in subdued voices underneath the organ prelude—and then you wonder why your mind wanders throughout the service.

As in sports, worship is a discipline in which there are no substitutes for time and practice. To be any good at it, we need to take time to prepare with our whole being: body, mind, soul. As we do this time after time, our practice may not make perfect, but it will certainly make better.

Corporate worship is a group experience, but also an individual exercise. When everyone is truly worshiping, the effect is absolutely energizing. When many are trapped into merely playing the role, it takes more effort for a worshiper to get involved in worship. One of the ways we can therefore stimulate our surrounding brothers and sisters in Christ to love and good works (see Heb. 10) is to help set the example which facilitates their worship.

Preparation for Worship

"Good idea," you say, "but how about some practical suggestions?" Here are several ways to give it the time and practice your corporate worship experience deserves:

- Ease back on Saturday evenings. With practice, such schedule adjustments become welcome sabbaticals from activity-filled lives. Help your family understand not only what you are doing, but why. Such preparation for worship is in itself an act of worship. If kids are slow out of the blocks in the mornings, maybe having them lay out their clothes and take baths the night before Sunday can ease pre-church tensions.

- Arrive at church with enough time to enable everyone to get where they need to be without stress. For some families—mine included—this is a genuine challenge, but it is worth the effort to get rolling sooner.

- Don't pick Sunday mornings as a time to resolve the prior week's family communication problems. Do that on Saturday.

- Take time for fellowship with other believers—that's part of the fun of getting together as God's children—but allow time also for personal preparation for worship. As the service start nears, gradually pull out of conversation and move into contemplation. After all, in worship God is the Audience and you are the performer. Get ready!

- Once the service begins, focus on making each facet an expression of worship to God. This is where the rubber meets the road. When the leader prays, you pray. Ignore the kid playing with keys in the next row. When the group sings, you sing, making each sentence a telegram from your heart to God's. Forget the off-key singing of the lady nearby. When the group gives, you give—without comparing your gift to the gentleman's just before you. Give with gratefulness that you have anything to give, since it comes to you first from God's hand. When the choir sings, worship with them. Don't count their noses or fret about their jewelry. They are there to help lead in worship; don't worry about the small stuff. When the sermon comes, you listen and respond in the ways you think God desires of you.

- When the service has ended, be less concerned about who greets you than about how you worshiped God. If you want to talk with someone, you take the initiative instead of expecting others to come to you.

Restoring Sunday to Sonday is, simply, a change of focus. But changing the object of our attention is not easy, just simple. Like the other aspects of lifestyle worship.

Chapter 22
Mastering Mammon

❧

Money is wonderful! Like dynamite, it has enormous potential. Like dynamite, it is dynamic; it can build and it can destroy. It can be a marvelous tool and a malicious master.

Anything with this range of capability needs to be handled cautiously. Can you spare a moment for some money questions? Ready or not, here they come:

Question $1: How would you describe your relationship to money?

Question $2: Is wealth a sign of God's approval of one's life?

Question $3: How can you make your money management an act of worship?

It has been my privilege to spend most of the last decade helping people in financial matters. Most often I assist in long-range planning, targeting goals from two years away to well beyond the lifetime of the individual(s) with whom I work.

It gets very personal at times. No two situations are identical, yet there are some concerns which emerge regularly.

So much could be said about so many areas of finances that my challenge in these few pages is what to omit, rather than what to include. Let's focus on several recurring long-range concerns and look at them through worship lenses.

Issue $1: God's Perspective on Money

First, money is a means, not an end. Read your newspaper, and on any given day you will find references to the salary received by this athlete, that businessman, or those actors. Periodic magazine surveys tabulate incomes by occupation. Over and over, our attention is drawn to how much money various people receive for various kinds of work. Little is said about how they use it.

The message is clear: Make as much money as you can. Little else matters. That's what others will look at as they decide how much respect to give you.

If you don't make a lot of money, forget respect regardless of what worthy things you do. If you do make a lot of money, count on high esteem no matter what else you do or how worthwhile your money-getting method was.

God's perspective, not surprisingly, is 180 degrees away from the world's. He says to disregard money, except as it contributes to your ability to truly give glory to Him. Show that money is not enshrined in your heart. Show that money is not your master, but that you are master of your money.

How? One way is to select your occupation based on how God has crafted you rather than on how much it will pay. Choose your career based on how well you think it will enable you to worship Him, given the way He has gifted and equipped you.

For one of many examples in the Bible, look at Moses who, "when he had grown up, refused to be known as the son of Pharaoh's daughter. He chose to be mistreated along with the people of God rather than to enjoy the pleasures of sin for a short time. He regarded disgrace for the sake of Christ as of greater value than the treasures of Egypt, because he was looking ahead to his reward" (Heb. 11:24-26).

Another way is to share generously with others in need. A negative example is the rich man clearly married to a lifestyle of the rich and famous (Luke 16:19-31). Lazarus, a homeless, poverty-stricken, sick and starving man, was laid at the entrance to the rich man's estate.

Receiving no help, the poor man died. Soon, so did the rich man.

Lazarus went to heaven, the rich man went to hell, and immediately their roles were reversed. The rich man begged from the fire of hell for a drop of water from Lazarus's finger. "No can do," refereed Abraham, and the rich, selfish man was condemned to unending agony.

Wealthy or not, God wants us to share with others in need. This is one way we show our love for God and for each other (John 13:35). It is one way we store up heavenly reward for ourselves (1 Tim. 6:17-19). That's a win-win-win situation—the best of all for all!

We can also dethrone money by treating those who are poor with the same respect—no more and no less—as we do those who are wealthy (James 2:1-9). That is rather radical and may raise a noble eyebrow or two.

Still another way to dethrone money in your heart is to simply give it away, not out of guilt, but out of joy that you are able to do so. Such giving—especially when no one knows and when no tax deduction is forthcoming—can be as personally refreshing as the jolt you get diving into a cool river after a hot afternoon of outside labor.

Why? Because we tend to be so selfish (the antithesis of worshiping God). We spend so much time using money to pay the bills, to cut the taxes, to impress, to acquire, to manipulate, to bargain, to control, to woo.

Why not, as Mary with her bottle of precious perfume, pour out an "I love You!" to God with no strings attached and with nothing in it for yourself? It's just counter-cultural enough to remind you of what's most important.

So . . . money is a means, not an end. "A means of what?" you ask. A means of lifestyle worship.

Second, money reveals our values. You could easily tell what is important to Jan and me just by looking at our checkbook entries. We could do the same with yours. Money flows toward our interests, doesn't it?

Conversely and interestingly, our hearts follow our funds also. Why? Perhaps partly because our expenditures reveal our hearts and partly because we haven't snubbed money enough.

Have you ever made an impulsive major purchase? It may have been a "great deal" on a marginally-beneficial time-share condo, an unnecessary new motor toy or _____ (you fill in the blank).

Did your attention not follow your expenditure? Suddenly you had another obligation to monitor and another acquisition from which to "get your money's worth."

God, of course, knows this connection between our hearts and our funds. Centuries ago, He said, "Do not store up for yourselves treasures on earth . . . but store up for yourselves treasures in heaven . . . for where your treasure is, there your heart will be also" (Matt. 6:19-21).

Third, God owns it all (Ps. 50:10; Job 1:21). Our wealth comes from Him as a gift (Eccl. 5:19) to be used for His glory (1 Peter 4:11*b*).

Have you ever heard other Christians talk as if 10 percent (or less) of their income is God's, but the rest of their income and all of their assets are their own? Wrong! It's all His. It's ours to manage for Him, but His to own (see Luke 19:11-27). And as is true of all managers, we are accountable to Him for our management of the whole tamale, not just the popular 10 percent.

That understanding has profound implications. Think about it.

Issue $2: *Our Perplexity Concerning Wealth*

Have you seen or heard any "prosperity preachers"? They glide down to a church, radio, or TV station from one of their several small mansions in one of their several ritzy cars to spread their gospel to all Christians who will contribute to their "ministry."

"God wants you to be healthy. God wants you to be wealthy. Just name it and claim it!"

I wonder how the apostle Paul would react were he to sit in with his friend, Dr. Luke, on one of these meetings. "Woe is me! Why didn't I hear this sooner? And to think I could have avoided all the painful floggings, that stoning which nearly took me out, the sleepless nights, the disgusting prisons, repeated deprivation of food and water, those shipwrecks—and my thorn in the flesh. All I had to do was name it and claim it and I could have enjoyed a happy, healthy life—and I could have been rich, rich, rich!"

Not a chance.

How about Jesus Christ? What, based on what you know about His earthly ministry, do you suppose He would say?

Most prosperity theology is a combination of wishful thinking, eisegesis or reading into Scripture things that really aren't there, and fundraising to support that preacher in the manner to which (s)he has become accustomed.

Citing such proverbs as "Prosperity is the reward of the righteous" (13:21) or "The generous man will prosper . . . " (11:25)—that's sure to get a few more bucks for the preacher. The proponents present proverbs as if they were promises. Moses, who also attends the meeting in spirit, is absolutely livid by now and looking for something stone-hewn to smash. John the Baptizer, who accompanied Moses and Paul on this excursion, rolls down the center aisle hooting and guffawing at the ludicrousness of it all.

"The one proverb this meeting verifies," says Dr. Luke to Paul under his breath, "is 'Like a lame man's legs that hang limp is a proverb in the mouth of a fool' "(26:7).

Proverbs are not time bound promises. They not only convey wisdom to the reader, but they also require wisdom by the reader.

For example, proverbs fundamentally support the New Testament teaching that we reap what we sow, but anyone who tries to force God into a timeline by saying that this reaping must come during one's earthly lifetime needs reality therapy.

Proverbs teach values. They show wise choices. They warn against real dangers. They provide wonderful instruction. But they are not time-bound promises.

The bottom line on prosperity theology is that spending any time or money on it is a poor investment of your life. Its history of dividends is atrocious.

Prosperity itself can be the pits. Matthew shows that money can produce enormous anxiety and, further, that it can take God's place as your master (6:24) if you let it get out of control.

Wannabes—erstwhile yuppies, dinks (double-income-no-kids), and so on—in pursuit of wealth also run great risks:

> People who want to get rich fall into temptation and a trap and into many foolish and harmful desires that plunge men into ruin and destruction. For the love of money is a root

of all kinds of evil. Some people, eager for money, have wandered from the faith and pierced themselves with many griefs. (1 Tim. 6:9-10)

Proverbs notwithstanding, perhaps you are relatively wealthy. Note that, while you may also have wealthy relatives, that is significantly different from being relatively wealthy! As mentioned above, your wealth is one of God's gifts to you—regardless of how it became yours.

You need to ask yourself at least two important questions: How much is "enough" for me? If I have more than "enough," what does God want me to do with it? Answers to both questions vary with each person and must be Spirit-led.

I know some very wealthy people who have apparently asked themselves those questions. Their resulting frugality might surprise you. They much prefer anonymity, so let me go to a well-known person of recent history for an example.

John Wesley grew up in poverty. When he followed his father into ministry, he had no reason to expect that his life would be any more prosperous than his dad's. However . . .

In 1731, he began to limit his expenses to free up more money for needy people. His cost of living was 28 pounds and income was 30 pounds, so he gave two pounds away.

The next year, his income doubled and he kept his expenses level, so he gave away 32 pounds. The following year, he earned 90 pounds and kept his expenses level, so he gave away 62 pounds.

This pattern continued as time moved along, and one year he earned 1,400 pounds. His expenses had by now mushroomed to an astounding 30 pounds, so what did he do that year? He gave away 1,370 pounds to needy people.[20]

Dramatically and with every opportunity to do otherwise, he practiced what he preached. For a Christian, increasing income should be accompanied by a rise in his or her standard of giving, not standard of living.

How pathetic his example makes the statement of a more recent member of the rich and famous elite, who responded to the question "How much is enough?" with "Just a little more."

Issue $3: The Principle of Contentment

One of the most challenging of money matters is control. Without even knowing you personally, I can say with reasonable certainty that controlling expenditures is a biggie for you.

Why? Because you are so strongly influenced by worshipless expectations, whether self-inflicted or imposed by significant others in your life. (See chapter 8, "Facing Up to Expectations," for a review of that influence.)

How do I know? I fight the same battles myself.

You are also influenced by unwarranted comparisons. (See chapter 12, "Keeping Up with the Joneses," for more about those.) Counter-worship comparisons and expectations are closely intertwined, and they also have in common the fact that the path to their satiation—if such is even possible—is paved with money. To relieve the tension we feel about this or that comparison or expectation, we throw money at it.

That, of course, is what makes control so difficult: We spend money on emotion far more often than on reason. Advertisers know this and explore it to the limit. It's a trap into which Satan delights to see Christians fall, since it wastes our money and reduces funds which could be channeled into much more spiritually productive directions.

Those whose income is variable fight an additional battle: controlling earnings plus expenditures. Again, how much is enough? When should I throttle back my work and give more time to other important areas of my life?

The key to control is contentment. Paul set the pace, saying that he had learned—the hard way, the term implies—to move easily from poverty to wealth without waste or pride and from wealth to poverty without envy or greed. How? By Christ's strength and help (Phil. 4:11-13).

Your control will be enhanced when emotional expenditures are ruled out. How can you rule them out? By the constant renewal of your mind by God. You can quench this transformation by His Spirit, or you can facilitate it. He wants to do it. The question is, do you?

Americans are fairly good readers. Most will recognize that the Bible says godliness plus contentment equals great gain (1 Tim. 6:6). Living it, however, is a different matter. Our lives too often preach that godliness plus great gain equals contentment!

Contentment implies balance. Your challenge and mine is to keep our "haves" and our "wants" in balance and under control.

Imagine a fulcrum. Balanced across this fulcrum is a board, and on one side is your "wants" inventory. On the other is your "haves" inventory.

If the inventories match, no problem. However, if "wants" exceed "haves," you can choose one of three options: first, maintain the imbalance and live discontentedly; second, acquire the wants and regain balance but lose control; or third, purge the wants, regain balance and control, and be content.

In lifestyle worship, each time the cycle recurs, we need to determine, as our "reasonable service of worship," which is the best "I love You!" we can offer to God.

Other passages you may wish to explore and ponder in this regard include Psalm 78:17-20; Proverbs 13:8; 17:1; 30:7-9; Ecclesiastes 4:4-8; 5:10-17; 1 Timothy 6; Hebrews 13:5; and 2 Peter 1:2-9.

Issue $4: The Priority of Planning

Planning is such a part of today's world that some Christians sincerely believe planning must be unspiritual. They feel it demonstrates a lack of faith in and dependence upon God. It seems downright carnal.

Not so. The text often cited in support of that position is "Therefore do not worry about tomorrow; for tomorrow will worry about itself. Each day has enough trouble of its own" (Matt. 6:34). Actually, Jesus says nothing here about planning. This abused verse is nested inside a ten-verse passage about anxiety.

Proverbs, as mentioned earlier, gives us general instruction and teaches important values. A brief look at several proverbs may be helpful now.

"Commit to the LORD whatever you do, and your plans will succeed" (Prov. 16:3). God blesses our work when we do it as worship to Him—and He assumes here that we have made plans.

Is that James I hear, asking "What good is it, my brothers, if a man claims to have faith but has no deeds? Can such faith save him?" (James 2:14).

"Make plans by seeking advice; if you wage war, obtain guidance" (Prov. 20:18). No denigration of planning here. God's point in this proverb is that we should make plans—and base them on good advice.

Other verses on which you may also meditate include Proverbs 21:5; 21:20; 30:25; Ecclesiastes 11:1–2.

Lifestyle worship is a thoughtful experience. It is "reasoned out." Planning—especially for important areas of life such as finances—must be welcomed as critical to the process of using our money worshipfully. The money, after all, is God's. Would you like Him to catch you, as the stewards in Jesus' parables, in the act of managing it or winging it?

Financial management includes meeting present and future needs. We should save systematically for future requirements and emergencies. We must manage risk through reasonable and appropriate insurance protection. We are also wise to save future money by maintaining what we now have, be it our hatchback, our house, or our health. Whatever the particular detail, God calls us to be good managers of what He gives us.

What we don't need—and sometimes what we do—should be given to needy others as part of our worship to God. This happens continuously throughout our life, a la Wesley. It also happens at our death, when we certainly will have no further need for funds. Think beyond the moment! Plan now.

❦

Money is a major aspect of life, but don't worry about it. Keep the basics in mind: the perspective of God, our perplexity about wealth, the principle of contentment, and the priority of planning.

As part of your unique lifestyle worship, you can count on God to lead you through the money maze effectively—if you allow Him.

Chapter 23
Extending Your Influence

❧

It was evening in San Diego. The harbor lights were beautiful as I drove along the shore, winding my way over to the airport terminal. I was picking up a friend who had flown in to see his terminally ill brother.

I couldn't help but smile when I finally saw Dick by the curb. We have only gotten together a few times in the past two decades—understandable when we live on separate continents!—but our friendship goes back over thirty-five years. My parents served with him as missionaries in South America, I went to school with his kids, and he knew me when I was ten years old. Always interested in people, Dick's friendship nourishes those he is near.

We loaded his luggage and threaded our way through the traffic, heading for the open highway. We talked as I drove, each catching the other up on life since our last visit.

I mentioned that I was writing a book about lifestyle worship. Immediately interested, he quizzed me further. After a few minutes, he sat back in the seat, looked out into the night, and then back at me.

"It doesn't surprise me at all that you are doing this book," he said. "Your folks lived just what you are writing about. They poured out their lives to others, using their gifts in worship."

Legacies. The first thought in my mind when he said that was, *Wow! I didn't think of this as part of their legacy to me. How like God to lead Dick to show me this connection, this continuity. How exciting to see my work as another extension of their influence!*

What lasting legacy will you leave?

As we begin life, every stage opens up new horizons, much like climbing a mountain slope. We go from the crib to the crawl. Then we stand, then walk, then run—and that opens up great new vistas: We can terrorize our parents until preschool puts us into the classroom!

Soon after preschool, we're in high school, and then comes college or career. We start out as an employee, move up to supervisor, leap into management, and perhaps even climb the leadership ladder. Then . . .

Horizons begin to shrink. No matter what the title, we know—and everyone else knows—that we have peaked, and are on our way downhill. To the sidelines.

The time comes when we can no longer run. Then walking becomes a challenge. Then standing falls aside. We find ourselves being tucked into a bed with rails. It looks a lot like a crib.

Life on earth is so brief, compared to eternity. How can we extend our influence? How can we leave a lasting legacy of worship?

Opportunities for Some

A number of possibilities exist for leveraging your lifestyle worship into long-term influence. Billy Graham and Charles Swindoll have done it through widely-disseminated preaching. A.W. Tozer and Charles Colson have leveraged their influence through writing. Bill Pearce and James Dobson have used radio media. Bill and Gloria Gaither have used music.

Leadership is another way to leverage impact. Think of the worldwide effect of such leaders as Dawson Trotman through The Navigators, Paul Fleming through New Tribes Mission, Bill Bright through Campus Crusade for Christ, and John Mitchell through Multnomah School of the Bible. Their use of their gifts in God's work is very much in keeping with the Romans 12 concept of lifestyle worship.

Teaching is another avenue of impact extension. Several years ago I strolled through a music exhibit hall. I happened to be in town at the same time as a national church music convention so I stopped by to see a few friends. Who found me was an even greater surprise than who I found.

As I checked out the various displays in the huge auditorium, I suddenly heard my name. "Mr. Garmo. Mr. Garmo! Over here!"

I turned around, lined up with the sound, and there across the aisle stood a young man who—I realized with a happy shock—had been my student a decade ago. What a thrill!

I had not known where Dave had gone after graduating from college, so seeing him now was a welcome and joyful surprise. Surprise became respect when I learned that he was now the director of marketing for one of the country's largest church music publishers.

After we talked for a few minutes, he said, "I want you to know something. You, perhaps more than any other person, are the reason I am here today. Your encouragement, your confidence that I had something to offer, kept me going."

His comments not only made my day; they made my year. Oh, for more students who can honestly say that to a teacher of theirs. What a privilege it is to teach, and in doing so, to help young men and women become who God designed them to be.

One problem, obviously, is that these opportunities are limited. God doesn't want all of us to preach or write or do radio or music. (Spare us, Lord, from that!) He doesn't give everyone the ability or the opportunity to lead ministries or teach school. He does, however, give some opportunities to everyone.

Opportunities for All

There are at least three ways we each can extend our influence: memories, mentees, and money trees.

Memories

A significant portion of my work involves time with retirees. A significant portion of that time is spent listening.

What do you suppose I hear most often? I hear them speak of memories. Memories about the way things were, about ways they have changed over the years and—note this—memories about the significant others in their life.

Are you a significant other to others? Probably so. Don't sell yourself short. Who are they?

The bad news is that we cannot control what memories others have of us. It's whatever they catch us in the act of doing. It's also whatever you and they do together—and that's where we can do something special about our legacy.

I enjoy hearing about my parents from people like Dick. I get the benefit of a different perspective from my own as their son. His memories of them, as you now know, are a great encouragement to me. His memories are part of their lasting legacy.

Will people have memories of you pouring out your love for God in thankful and fulfilling service to others? Will they remember you abiding—hanging tightly to Him—in good times and bad?

Memories can be triggered by other means. A photograph, a song, a journal of blessings kept during hard times, a visit to places where you worshiped God in one special way or another. Done sincerely—without hypocrisy—memory making is a wonderful way to extend your influence by putting pictures of lifestyle worship into other minds, to be replayed over and over in the years ahead.

Mentees

Paul said, "And the things you have heard me say . . . entrust to reliable men who will also be qualified to teach others" (2 Tim. 2:2).

Discipling others has been an important stimulus to the Christian walk of thousands of believers. It is an outstanding way to grow and fellowship.

Another application of this verse is similar, yet distinct from discipling. It is mentoring.

As a discipler, you can help another person develop the disciplines of a worshiper of God. As a mentor, you can provide modeling, close supervision on special projects, and personal help in areas of life needing encouragement, correction, confrontation, or accountability.

A mentor is a wise and trusted counselor who is willing to help a less experienced person reach his or her goals. A mentee, also known as the protege, is the person being helped by the mentor.

Mentoring is simply the process of making the mentor's personal strengths, resources, and network available to help the mentee reach his or her goals. The purpose is to more fully develop the mentee, not to reproduce a clone of the mentor.

The process can be structured any way the mentor and mentee wish around the core question: "How can I help you reach your goals today?" Typically, they discuss upcoming decisions to be made, problems to be addressed, plans, progress since their last meeting, prayer requests, and other concerns. This is all related to goals in such areas of life as family, finances, professional development, or spiritual development.

A mentee may have different mentors for various areas of life goals. The relationship may be lifelong or limited. Mentoring, whatever form it takes, is a way for you to extend your lifestyle worship influence.

Bobb Biehl and Glen Urquhart wrote a quick-start orientation and guidance booklet entitled "Mentoring," which you will find helpful.[21] Another excellent source is *The Fine Art of Mentoring*, a book written by Dr. Ted W. Engstrom.

Money Trees

Conventional wisdom says money doesn't grow on trees, but I know differently. I've seen money trees!

From time to time as our church celebrated a special occasion for a special person, the group would give the person a card, a few small presents, and a money tree. Perhaps the money tree was the most practical of all, since it could take the form of anything the receiver needed.

Imagine that all your assets, including your home, your life insurance, and your china closet, were converted into cash and put on a money tree. How do you want it distributed when you die? Who would get how much?

Part of extending your influence is planning your estate in such a way that needs are cared for and God is glorified. This is not just for the wealthy. We all need to do it and have the opportunity to do it in a way that clearly honors God.

It is a given that all the assets God has temporarily entrusted to you must someday be released to others. The nagging question as manager—God is the Owner—is who should get what.

The Bible gives us two guidelines for determining this distribution. One is love. God set the example personally: "For God so loved . . . that he gave . . ." (John 3:16). His example holds whether our giving is to Him or to those He loves so much (see Matt. 27:37-40).

Another guideline for giving is need. Any friends or family members who have been dependent on you during your life will need continuing support when you head home to heaven.

"If anyone does not provide for his relatives, and especially for his immediate family, he has denied the faith and is worse than an unbeliever" (1 Tim. 5:8). God's condemnation here upholds the importance of providing for such dependents as minor children, aged parents, spouses and ministry interests.

Note that this verse does not talk about prospering dependents, but about providing for them; and it is silent about those who have grown up and left the household. The critical difference is dependency.

For some people, a third reason for giving is tradition. They distribute part or all of their assets to a person because they feel some vague sense of obligation. Do you sense that pull as you consider your own estate planning?

As Christians, we need to examine such a "reason" carefully, prayerfully, and critically. God clearly declared His motivation for giving to us: love.

He is just as clear about what He wants our motivation to be: love (1 Cor. 13). In fact, He scorns gifts given to Him for tradition's sake (Matt. 15:3-9). If our giving plan disregards or misstates God's desires for our stewardship of His assets, of what value is all our sophisticated planning?

Have you completed your planning in this regard?

If you don't have a will or a revocable living trust, I have some good news and some bad news. The good news is that your state loves you and has a wonderful plan for your estate.

The bad news is that its plan may be worlds away from yours and God's, denying some who needed you and giving to others whose lifestyle you had no intention of supporting. Meanwhile, you will have crossed the bridge over which you cannot return to straighten things out.

Get your own plan into place. It will be your last chance to manage anything of value on earth and one of your final opportunities to extend your godly influence. Why give that privilege to people you don't even know?

Once done, it's a good idea to review your plan every three years or so to be certain it is up-to-date. Many think this is good advice, but few mark their calendars! Be different: Do it.

"Sure," you say. "But what do I do?" Here are some suggestions which may help you whether you are initiating or reviewing your estate plan:

- List your loved ones and dependent people. Remember to include your ministry interests, because of your love for them and the God they serve and because of their dependence upon you.
- List your property, that is, your transferable assets. Include their approximate market value and then convert them to cash in your mind and put that cash onto a money tree.
- Ask your heavenly Father how He would want that tree given away if you were to die today.

Here is a nine-point checklist you may use as you make or review your plans:

1. Have you reviewed your estate arrangements within the past three years? Are there any substantial changes in people, property or plans?

2. Is your plan built on the recognition that God owns it all? Does it reflect your management of His assets?

3. Do you have a durable power of attorney to manage property and make crucial health decisions in case you become incompetent prior to death?

4. Have you provided for guardianship and property management for minor children?

5. Is the ownership of your property coordinated with your estate documents? This is often where problems arise.

6. Have you included a letter of instructions for the distribution of household goods and personal effects?

7. Have you done everything possible to avoid interpersonal conflicts among family members?

8. Have you considered the benefits of using a revocable living trust?

9. Are you now completely satisfied with your existing estate plan?

Leaving a Lasting Legacy

Did you ever wish you could give something away twice, instead of having to choose one beneficiary over another? Many Christians experience an estate distribution dilemma as they try to give both to family and to ministry interests.

There are several ways to resolve this, but we'll take time now for just one interesting solution. Let's suppose you have some stocks and bonds.

Rather than giving them directly to family beneficiaries, you put them into a charitable trust. You tell the trustee to give the trust's earned income to family until that income equals the initial value of the property. Afterward, the property is directed to your ministry interest.

What happens? If the property produces a 10 percent return per year, the trust terminates in a decade, having paid your family 100 percent of the initial trust value over the years. Your ministry interest then receives 100 percent of the terminating trust value. Sometimes you can have your cake and eat it too!

My parents' legacy was not money. They had none, and if it were there it would have been second-best at best. What they gave us kids was far more valuable: a love for God, two marvelous models of abiding, and a heart for serving.

Again, what will *your* legacy be?

❦

A wall closes the far end of the hallway of portraits. On it hangs another portrait. If you stand at the entrance to the hallway and gaze down to its end, you see this person looking back at you.

Suddenly you realize, as you check portraits on both sides of the corridor, that no matter which side they are on, the faces are turned toward that portrait at the end. It is as if they are all looking to Jesus. So, too, shall we in our final section.

Part 5:
GAZING UPWARD

Rather, clothe yourselves
   with the Lord Jesus Christ,
   and do not think about how to gratify
   the desires of the sinful nature.
Now to him who is able to establish you
   . . . to the only wise God,
   be glory forever
   through Jesus Christ! Amen.
   (Romans 13:14; 16:25, 27)

Chapter 24

Looking to Jesus

❧

He began so well. Young, handsome, strong, and towering a full head above everyone around him, he was a real hunk. Malcom had it all—and a wealthy, influential father as well. What a guy! What a situation! And he loved God.

His rise to prominence came early. Singled out before reaching full adulthood to become his country's chief executive, Malcom at first was so overwhelmed at the prospect of leading his country that he ran away.

He was later found hidden on his father's huge ranch. Finally coaxed out of seclusion, he accepted his fate and began preparing for his enormous leadership role.

Malcom had no opposition as he assumed his highly visible and important position. He enjoyed his widespread public support. Everything seemed to be going so well.

Then something changed. Observers reported an occasion on which Malcom usurped the role of his country's principal religious authority. This was a major incident, since religion was a dominant force in Malcom's country.

The news got progressively worse. A group of religious leaders who opposed him were found murdered in their church building. Later reports identified Malcom and his troops as the mass murderers.

In another crisis, instead of looking to God at a time of crisis, he consulted a medium. So much for abiding.

These and other developments contributed to Malcom's demise. Increasingly unstable, he became a torment to himself and those around him. He defied the God he had so readily acknowledged when his public career began.

Warnings were useless. Confronted repeatedly, his erratic responses only underscored his spiritual decay.

Finding himself eventually in an international war which he knew would trap him in the jaws of defeat, Malcom committed suicide. Amid total disaster, he died surrounded by death.

Michael, too, began so well. Like Malcom, he began humbly. The youngest of a large family, he too was discovered out in his father's fields, running toward—not from—responsibility.

Chosen, as Malcom, to become his country's next chief executive, he proved himself capable in every way. He was young, handsome, and strong. What a guy! What a situation! And he loved God.

Among Michael's greatest tests was the intense, prolonged and malicious opposition from the ruling administration. They did not want to relinquish their power and prestige. Yet, in challenge after challenge he responded with godly judgment and uncanny ability.

Religion was a prominent influence in his country, and Michael set the pace for his people. When the time finally came for him to assume his high public office, he proclaimed his love for God by taking a proactive role in establishing and enhancing the spiritual vitality of his nation.

He complemented, not usurped, the work of his appointed religious leaders. During his administration, their ministry flourished as never before.

He enjoyed widespread support. Everything seemed to be going so well.

Then something changed. Virile man that Michael was, he succumbed to the beauty of a married woman who was not his wife.

Compounding the tragedy of adultery was the tragedy of murder. Michael coldly arranged for the death of his lover's husband. It gets worse: The betrayed husband and murder victim happened to be one of Michael's most devoted employees.

This incongruous debacle had to stop. Finally—and carefully—the country's key clergyman confronted Michael. Wielding a few disarmingly simple, well-selected sentences with the skill of a surgeon, he cut through Michael's facade and exposed the ugly truth.

It was a supremely significant moment. How would this powerful and charismatic leader react to such serious charges?

Michael's response was 180 degrees from Malcom's. Instead of usurping this daring spiritual leader's authority, and instead of murdering him a la Malcom, he fell on his face in repentance. Not just privately, but publicly he confessed his sin to God and the people.

Michael's grief-filled repentance was rewarded with God's gracious forgiveness. To be sure, he had to cope with the consequences of his failure. But he also experienced the comfort of God's faithfulness.

God resumed His work in and through a renewed and restored Michael, and when the time came for him to move onward to heaven, he left under the best of circumstances. Having enjoyed long life, wealth and honor, he died surrounded by caring family and friends.

Our Voyage of Lifestyle Worship

The real names of these two people, as you may have guessed, are Saul and David. Their royally fascinating stories are reported in the Old Testament books of Samuel and Chronicles.

Saul and David had goals not unlike yours and mine. Their beginnings were modest. They probably dreamed of someday becoming significant.

As adults, they each clearly wanted to maximize their potential. Likewise, they were both drawn to meaningful living rather than mediocre survival. They sought challenge and adventure and experienced their share of set-backs.

How do you account for the critical difference in their lives? Their endings were as divergent as their beginnings were similar. What can you and I learn from them?

Suppose, early one morning, you go out to sea in a small boat. The weather is great, the day is young, and the water looks like sculptured blue carpet. You venture further.

As if on cue, the weather turns. Winds begin to blow, bringing clouds that block out the sun and a chill that penetrates to your bones. Waves get bigger and bigger, emerging out of the water like terrifying clones of the Loch Ness monster.

It's so foggy that you can hardly tell mist from ocean. You're not sure where to head.

Then you see it. Barely visible at first, you still recognize and respond. Filled with relief and thankfulness, you turn your boat toward the lighthouse on the shore.

Fog continues to roll over you. Waves still toss your craft around like a T-shirt in a clothes dryer. Your very bone marrow is still chilled.

But it's okay now! With your eyes focused on the lighthouse, your hands, arms, and feet automatically do what they're supposed to do. Not long thereafter, you successfully skipper your ship to the warmth and safety of port.

God is our beacon. If we look to Him, we avoid shipwreck. That is the supreme lesson of Mary, Hannah, Paul, Jehoshaphat, and many others before us. It is He who makes something beautiful out of our lives.

In this voyage of lifestyle worship, Jesus is not only our Goad, but our Guide. He is not only our Model, but our Mentor. He is not only our Encourager, but our Enabler. "I am the way and the truth and the life. No one comes to the Father except through me" (John 14:6).

Jeremiah understood it well:

> "Let not a wise man boast of his wisdom or the strong man boast of his strength or the rich man boast of his riches, but let him who boasts boast about this: that he understands and knows me, that I am the LORD who exercises kindness, justice and righteousness on earth, for in these I delight," declares the LORD. (Jer. 9:23-24)

A Shower of Scripture

Founded as lifestyle worship is on God's Word, we can do no better than to end our study with an unhurried look at God's Word. Would you like to find a quiet place and give your heart a shower of Scripture?

The following portions of Scripture are drawn from the chapters of this book. Taken together, this collage is like a musical finale which recapitulates in one medley melodies presented earlier in the composition. May it encourage you to turn your eyes upon Jesus.

Blessed is the man who does not walk in the counsel of the wicked or stand in the way of sinners or sit in the seat of mockers. But his delight is in the law of the LORD, and on his law he meditates day and night. He is like a tree planted by streams of water, which yields its fruit in season and whose leaf does not wither. Whatever he does prospers. (Ps. 1:1-3)

He will have no fear of bad news; his heart is steadfast, trusting in the LORD. (Ps. 112:7)

Come, let us bow down in worship, let us kneel before the LORD our Maker. (Ps. 95:6)

Therefore, I urge you, brothers, in view of God's mercy, to offer your bodies as living sacrifices, holy and pleasing to God—which is your spiritual worship. (Rom. 12:1)

Therefore, since we are receiving a kingdom that cannot be shaken, let us be thankful, and so worship God acceptably with reverence and awe. (Heb. 12:28)

After removing Saul, he made David their king. He testified concerning him: "I have found David son of Jesse a man after my own heart; he will do everything I want him to do." (Acts 13:22)

Jesus replied: " 'Love the Lord your God with all your heart and with all your soul and with all your mind' . . . Love your neighbor as yourself.' All the Law and the Prophets hang on these two commandments." (Matt. 22:37-40)

I am the vine; you are the branches. If a man remains in me and I in him, he will bear much fruit; apart from me you can do nothing. (John 15:5)

But the fruit of the Spirit is love, joy, peace, patience, kindness, goodness, faithfulness, gentleness and self-control. (Gal. 5:22-23)

May the God who gives endurance and encouragement give you a spirit of unity among yourselves as you follow Christ Jesus, so that with one heart and mouth you may glorify the God and Father of our Lord Jesus Christ. (Rom. 15:5-6)

For we are God's workmanship, created in Christ Jesus to do good works, which God prepared in advance for us to do. (Eph. 2:10)

Each one should use whatever gift he has received to serve others, faithfully administering God's grace in its various forms. (1 Peter 4:10)

I counsel you to buy from me . . . salve to put on your eyes, so you can see. (Rev. 3:18)

So whether you eat or drink or whatever you do, do it all for the glory of God. (1 Cor. 10:31)

And let us consider how we may spur one another on toward love and good deeds. (Heb. 10:24)

Submit to one another out of reverence for Christ. (Eph. 5:21)

You are not your own; you were bought at a price. Therefore honor God with your body. (1 Cor. 6:19b-20)

Be imitators of God . . . and live a life of love, just as Christ loved us and gave himself up for us as a fragrant offering and sacrifice to God. (Eph. 5:1-2)

I have learned the secret of being content in any and every situation. . . . I can do everything through him who gives me strength. (Phil. 4:12-13)

[Jehoshaphat said] "We have no power to face this vast army that is attacking us. We do not know what to do, but our eyes are upon you." (2 Chron. 20:12)

NOTES

1. Dwight Bradley, excerpted from *Leaves from a Spiritual Notebook*, Thomas S. Kepler, ed. (New York: Abingdon Press, 1960), 261.

2. William Temple, *Readings in St. John's Gospel* (Ridgefield, CT: Morehouse Publishing Co., 1985), 119.

3. Alfred North Whitehead, *Science and the Modern World*, Lowell Lectures, 1925 (New York: Macmillan, 1925), 192.

4. Temple, 119

5. Frank Minirth, Paul Meier, and Don Hawkins, *Worry-free Living* (Nashville, TN: Thomas Nelson Publishers, 1989), 165.

6. There is no universal agreement on precise distinctions between the terms "anxiety," "angst," and "worry." Some use the terms almost interchangeably. For example, the title of the above book by Minirth implies that "worry" will be examined throughout the treatise. In fact, it focuses on "anxiety."

For the purposes of this presentation, let us assume that worry is a form of focused anxiety, such as worry about what our children will do if we aren't watching them or what people will think if we don't buy the status symbols they revere. Let us also assume that anxiety and angst are interchangeable terms.

7. Roy Grinker, "Perspectives on Normality," *Archives of General Psychiatry* (1967) 17:257.

8. See Minirth above.

9. Cirilla D. Martin, *"Accepted in the Beloved."* Copyright © 1930. Renewal 1958 by Hope Publishing Co., Carol Stream, IL 60188. All rights reserved. Used by permission.

10. Gail Sheehy, *Passages:* (New York. Bantam, 1984).

11. Helen H. Lemmel, *"Turn Your Eyes Upon Jesus"* © 1922 Singspiration Music / ASCAP. All rights reserved. Used by permission of Benson Music Group.

12. Peter Francese and John Naisbitt, *The Experts' Guide to the Baby Boomers* (New York: Time, Inc., 1985), pp. 9, 23.

13. See Abraham H. Maslow, *Toward a Psychology of Being* (New York: Van Nostrand Reinhold, 1968). Another Maslow book on the same subject is *Farther Reaches of Human Nature* (New York: Viking Press, 1971).

14. Michael D. Taylor, "How to solve search and selection problems: Looking beyond job performance," *Motivation and Productivity* (Seattle: People Management Group International, introductory issue), 3.

15. C. Peter Wagner, *Your Spiritual Gifts Can Help Your Church Grow* (Glendale, CA: Regal Books, 1974).

16. Margaret E. Broadly, *Your Natural Gifts: How to recognize and develop them for success and self-fulfillment* (McLean, VA: EPM Publications, Inc., 1986), 155.

17. For example, see Bob Phillips, *The Delicate Art of Dancing with Porcupines* (Ventura, CA: Regal Books, 1989).

18. For more information, write to People Management Group International, 230 Nettleton Hollow Road, Washington CT. 06793.

19. Carol Hyatt and Linda Gottlieb, *When Smart People Fail: Rebuilding Yourself for Success* (New York: Viking Penguin, 1988).

20. Charles Edward White, "What Wesley Practiced and Preached About Money," *Leadership* 8, 1, (1987) 27.

21. To receive the booklet, "Mentoring," write to Bobb Biehl, Masterplanning Group International, P.O. Box 6128, Laguna Niguel, CA 92677.

TAKING TIME TO REFLECT
(Questions for Reflection and Discussion)

Chapter 2 - Turning Points

1. Think through the broad strokes of your life. How have you responded to important high points?

2. How have you responded to significant setbacks?

3. What effect did those have on your relationship with God?

4. Which scripture verses has God brought to your attention during your more difficult times?

5. Which Bible heroes came to your attention during these times? Why?

6. What three particularly memorable things did friends do for you when they discovered that you were going through deep waters?

Chapter 3 - Discovering the Essence

1. How would you define *worship* to a child?

2. Being brutally honest, if you imagine your life as a pie comprised of various slices (health, finances, family, career, etc.) is worship (a) one slice of the pie, (b) the center of the pie, or (c) nowhere to be seen?

3. How has worship affected your career?

4. How has worship influenced your self-concept?

5. How has worship affected your relationships?

6. Of all the verses in scripture about worship, which one or two rank as your favorites? Why?

7. Of all the men and women in scripture whose lives somehow demonstrate worship, which one or two are your favorites? Why?

8. Given that worship is directed toward God, either answer the following question in writing or discuss it with a friend: "What's in it for me?"

Chapter 4 - Living in Style

1. What written or unwritten lists of dos and don'ts have you used to stimulate your walk with Christ? Take time now to think them through and write them down. Why is each there?

2. Contrast the "holy walk" list of Colossians 2:20-23 with God's list in Colossians 3:1-17. What are the key differences?

3. Compare and contrast your lists with the 2 in question two. Which is yours most like? What insight does this give you about what glorifies and pleases God and what doesn't?

4. How does love counteract the negative effects of mere lists?

5. Consider love, as described in 1 Corinthians 13. Under what circumstances does the candle of love shine brightest? What implications does this have for us as we express the worship of loving God?

6. Love IS a many splendored thing. What are several ways we can nurture and live out our worship of loving Him?

7. What do you suppose are two or three consequences precipitated by a person who focuses on serving God and minimizes or ignores the worship of loving Him and abiding in Him?

8. Some areas of abiding, such as waiting for His answers, are mentioned in this chapter. What other examples of abiding can you add?

9. Review the fruit of His Spirit in us which you find in 1 Corinthians 13:4-7 and Galatians 5:22-23. Reflect on instances in which each has shown in your life over the past month.

10. Think through each character quality again, this time reflecting on how it has shown in someone else's life sometime in the past six months because (in part) of your ministry to him/her. (Don't be self-conscious about this. You are not glorifying yourself; you are glorifying God's work through you. Give thanks with a grateful heart!)

Chapter 5 - Loving Devotedly

1. When do you tend to be more like Martha than Mary?

2. In what past two situations have you succumbed to complexity instead of focused on simplicity? How did it affect your effectiveness at those times?

3. "Lifestyle worship welcomes heart, not formula." What's wrong with formula worship?

4. What are some examples of formula worship?

5. "Lifestyle worship is daring, not dull." What is so daring about lifestyle worship?

6.   "Lifestyle worship focuses on giving, not receiving." In what ways is this like and unlike your current lifestyle?

7.   What personal steps can you take to express your unique "I love You!" to your heavenly Father?

Chapter 6 - *Abiding Resolutely*

1.   What two or three times do you recall, as with Hannah and Peninnah, being more focused on what you did NOT have than what you DID?

2.   What differences does that focus make?

3.   Why do you think God allows bad things to happen to good people?

4.   When are our problems the result of sin in our lives? And when are they not?

5.   What name for God did Hannah use as she prayed? What implications does this name—and this God— have for the key problem you are facing?

6.   When, as Hannah, have you bargained with God during a crisis? Did you honor your promise to Him, as Hannah, did with Samuel, or have you "forgotten" it?

7.   Imagine that you were Hannah or Elkanah, and gave Samuel away as a child. What conflicting thoughts would you experience in such a situation?

8.   How does the worship of abiding relate to the issue of faith-versus-works? Where in your life have you been—or are you being—tested in these areas of your spiritual pilgrimage?

9.   Meditate on what 1 John 2:24-29 says about abiding. What specific implications does this have for your life?

Chapter 7 - *Serving Effectively*

1.   As interviewed, Paul describes certain features of his personality and shows how God seemed to take that into consideration as He led Paul. How would you describe your personality?

2.   How has God seemed to consider your personality in leading you?

3.   Paul's view of ministry success seems at odds with prevalent opinions today. How would you compare and contrast the two?

4.   Supporting your response with scripture, what would you say is God's perspective on ministry success?

5.   Have you ever felt benched by God? If so, when?

6.   What can you learn in your life from Paul's period of obscurity following his conversion experience?

7.   Review, in the "interview" or in scripture, how God equipped Paul for his ministry. How has God equipped you for yours?

8.   Is Jesus really the Lord of your life? Does it show?

Chapter 8 - *Facing Up to Expectations*

1.   What unrealistic expectations have you imposed on yourself?

2.   How did these become your expectations?

3. What unrealistic expectations have you allowed others to impose on you?

4. Which were too high? Too wide? Too narrow? Off track?

5. In what areas have you complicated your life unnecessarily?

6. How can you modify these expectations into REASONABLE targets?

Chapter 9 - Getting Back to Basics

1. Like Cain, Abel's brother, we each are tempted to treat some formalities as if they were worship. Which ones are you inclined to perform mechanically?

2. What can you do to keep those rituals meaningful?

3. Compare Matthew 15:8-9 to today's Christian culture, noting examples of that passage being practiced today.

    With the quotation on worship from William Temple in mind, discuss the next three questions with an interested friend.

4. How can worship quicken your conscience?

5. How can worship nourish your mind?

6. How can worship purify your imagination?

7. In what personal or public way has your worship of God caused you to "dare to be different" in the past year?

8. What have you given—no strings attached—to God, as a sacrifice of worship?

Chapter 10 - Taking Aim at Angst

1. Which burdens bother you more, concerns about your past or concerns about your future?

2. Write out your top three anxieties on the lefthand side of a sheet of paper. On the righthand side put an X by those for which anxiousness will accomplish nothing.

3. By those that you can do something about, write down two actions you can take to relieve/reduce that concern.

4. If you are feeling anxious about action decisions you are considering, ask yourself for each, "What is the worst that can happen if I do (or do not) take this action?"

5. For each worst-case scenario, could you handle it if it occurred?

6. Pray through your anxieties, confessing and committing concerns to God wherever needed.

Chapter 11 - Turning Worry into Worship

1. How worry-prone are you, compared to most other people you know?

2. Compared to others in your frame of reference, how desirous are you of status symbols (impressive cars, clothes, furnishings etc.)? Compared to others, how often do you draw attention to your accomplishments? How often do you engage in name-dropping?

What do your responses tell you about your relative level of insecurity?

3.   Review the description in this chapter of a "Type A" personality. To what extent do you fit that description? What does that suggest about your vulnerability to high anxiety?

4.   Where are you in birth order, relative to your brothers and sisters? To what extent does the firstborn among you fit the general description summarized in this chapter? What effect do you suppose your birth order has had on anxiety in your life?

5.   Ask a good friend what defense mechanisms you tend to use when contemplating actions which may increase anxiety in your life.

6.   How would you explain to a friend that the worship of abiding helps control anxiety?

7.   Go thoughtfully through the suggestions for relieving anxiety which occur in the last half of the chapter. Apply them to your life where appropriate.

Chapter 12 - *Keeping up with the Joneses*

1.   Review the opening paragraphs describing the corporate ladder-climbers, scheming attorneys, competing sales force, and manipulative managers. Which of these scenarios have you personally observed or experienced?

2.   What INCOMPLETE comparisons do you find yourself making between others and yourself?

3.   What INCONGRUENT comparisons do you make between others and yourself?

4. How have those unhealthy comparisons affected you? Take them to the throne.

5. How much time do you suppose your mind dwells on the eternals in a given day? How has your answer affected your day-to-day living?

6. Review the progression from confused values to confused goals to . . . frustrated insignificance. Have you been victimized by this progression? What specific steps can you take to break out of it?

7. Spend a few thoughtful minutes reflecting on each excerpt from scripture quoted in this chapter.

Chapter 13 - Becoming a Nonconformist

1. Knowing your personality and tendencies, how do you imagine you would have responded to the news that Jehoshophat received regarding the imminent invasion of Judah?

2. Prayer is central to the worship of abiding. Read Jehoshophat's prayers in 2 Chronicles 20. What impresses you about them?

3. List two or three panics that have hit your life recently.

4. Each time, how did you respond?

5. How might you have "turned your eyes upon Jesus" in each circumstance?

6. Read for yourself the following passages, noting the recurring "Stand fast" theme and variations: 2 Chronicles 20; John 15; Ephesians 6:13-14. In what ways

do you think God would be honored for you to stand fast this next month?

Chapter 14 - *Being All That You Can Be*

1. Whether or not you are a baby-boomer, which characteristics (as described in this chapter) do you share with boomers?

2. Can we be truly self-actualized on earth?

3. Can we be self-actualized apart from God?

4. Was Jesus Christ self-actualized on earth?

5. You may be familiar with other theories of humanistic psychology than Maslow's. How do they deal with the reality of eternity?

6. How would you respond to a person steeped in psychology who asked you why Christianity should be considered as an orientation to living?

Chapter 15 - *Fulfilling Your Call*

1. What spiritual gift(s) do you have? How has your giftedness been confirmed?

2. What natural gifts do you have? What anecdotal evidence from your life underscores these gifts? Take time to write down your history of successes and joys; it is a very revealing and encouraging step to understanding who you are.

3. As presented in this chapter or elsewhere, how would you describe your social style?

4. Do you find yourself drawn more toward full-time ministry or marketplace ministry? Explain ("Because . . .").

5. Share your design with a good friend (starting with your spouse if you're married). Invite his or her input. Maybe he or she will find it helpful to do the same with you.

6. Based on your understanding of the way God designed you, how well does your current job use your personality and gifts?

7. Based upon your design, what should you—or should you not—be doing?

8. What expectations have lured—or threatened to lure— you away from fulfilling your design?

9 How has the "Peter Principle" affected you, or someone you know?

10. What steps should you take, vocationally and avocationally, to develop an overall environment in which you can praise God by better fulfilling His design for you?

Chapter 16 - Burning Out for God

1. Having high expectations is good—up to a point. When do they put a person in danger of burnout?

2. To which level of expectations (general, professional, or personal) do you feel most vulnerable?

3. Are you experiencing sustained situational stresses which affect you negatively?

4. How emotionally demanding is your work?

5. The contribution of oversupervision to burnout should catch the attention of managers and also of parents. Are you pushing someone toward burnout in either role?

6. Nourishing friendships can play an important part in both the prevention and cure of burnout. How would you characterize your friendships?

7. Look through the Bible and, of the many friendships described, identify three you regard as nourishing.

8. How does contentment relate to burnout?

9. Explain the relationship of forgiveness to burnout.

10. Consider where you are regarding loving Him, abiding in Him, and serving Him. Is your lifestyle worship balanced?

Chapter 17 - *Coping with Failure*

1. How can deferred gratification stir up a feeling of failure?

2. Summarize in your own words several key causes of failure.

3. How is failure a door to success?

4. How does the perspective that failure is an experience, rather than a trait, affect your understanding of failure?

5. What is the most notable "failure" you have yet experienced?

6. How did you respond to it?

7. What did you learn from it?

8. In what way(s) can that experience become a bridge to more loving, better abiding, or more effective serving?

Chapter 18 - *Making a Difference*

1. Have you ever felt trapped into merely making a living?

2. What, in your words, does it mean to "make a difference"?

3. How have two or three particular people made a difference in your life?

4. How do you think you have made a difference in the lives of two or three others?

5. If you feel you haven't made much of a difference, what obstacles have hindered you?

6. What new possibilities for making a difference in your work do you now see for yourself?

Chapter 19 - *Managing to Worship*

1. What, in your words, are two or three key distinctions of worship-filled management?

2. What, in your opinion, are the potential costs (to the manager) of worshipful management?

3. What are the potential gains to the organization?

4. How do you imagine non-Christian employees would respond to worshipful management?

5. Of the various characteristics of "managing ourselves" presented in this chapter, which two are most like you? Which two are least like you?

6. Of the various characteristics of "managing others" presented in this chapter, which two are most like you? Which two are least like you?

7. If you are a manager (at work, at home, or in avocational activities), what three steps can you take to make your managing more a reflection of your lifestyle worship?

Chapter 20 - *Living It at Home*

1. How is marriage like a small ship going out to sea?

2. If you are married, is your marriage a triangle? Who or what is at its apex?

3. What single change can you make in your own attitude or behavior that will show your spouse who's at the apex?

4. In what ways can/should we manage (i.e., be stewards of) our marriage relationship?

5. Describe in some detail what happens when we don't manage our marriage.

6. If you have children, what is the most important gift you can give them?

7. What steps are you taking to make that happen?

Chapter 21 - *Restoring Sunday to Sonday*

1. How is your worship when you are in church?

2. If you worship at church on Sunday, what single change in routine can you make on Saturday evening that will help the Sunday service become a more worshipful event?

3. How often do you get to church with enough time before services and classes to eliminate the tension of being late? If adjustments are needed, what, specifically are they?

4. If you are married, and especially with children, are your Sunday morning conversations and attitudes at home and on the way to church conducive to peace or closer to pandemonium? How might you manage pre-worship atmosphere better?

5. What were you thinking about during the most recent hymn or chorus you sang in church?

6. What were you thinking about during the most recent prayer offered?

7. What else can you practice to improve your group worship experience?

Chapter 22 - Mastering Mammon

1. What have you done to show your mastery over Mammon, versus Mammon's mastery over you?

2. How much money is enough for you?

3. If you have more than enough money, what do you think God wants you to do with the excess?

4. What role does contentment (or the lack thereof) play in your current financial situation?

5.   What is your position on the question of planning versus faith?

6.   At the end of the sections on contentment and planning are additional verses which relate to those issues. Ponder their relevance to your personal financial situation and your attitudes toward money.

Chapter 23 - Extending Your Influence

1.   What memories do you have of others which remind you of their love for God?

2.   In whom are you creating memories of your love for God?

3.   Whom has discipled you over the years? How?

4.   Whom has mentored you? How?

5.   Whom have you discipled?

6.   Who have you mentored?

7.   Who might you mentor?

8.   How does your estate plan reflect your love for God?

9.   What lasting legacies will you leave? How can you extend your godly influence?

Chapter 24 - Looking to Jesus

1.   Attitudinally, how are you similar to Saul?

2.   Likewise, how are you similar to David?

3. What implications do your answers have for your life? Discuss these with a good friend.

4. How is Jesus your Goad?

5. How is Jesus your Guide?

6. How is He your Mentor?

7. How is He your Enabler?

8. In what ways will you look to Jesus this week?

About the Author

John (Skip) Garmo is a missionary kid who grew up in two disparate jungles: Bolivia, South America, and Los Angeles, California.

Skip describes himself as "a recovering non-worshiper." He brings a broad experience to the challenge of Lifestyle Worship with his background in ministry, education, finance, music, and cross-cultural missions. His graduate study includes a Ph.D. with a major in psychomusicology.

Since 1988, Skip has served as Vice-President of MAF Foundation, a ministry of Mission Aviation Fellowship. He and Jan, his wife of over twenty-five years, live in California with their three teenagers, Byron, Krista, and Kara.